NO ONE HAS MORE LOVE THAN THIS...

WHY WE REMEMBER

WARREN ROBINSON

authorHOUSE

AuthorHouse™
1663 Liberty Drive
Bloomington, IN 47403
www.authorhouse.com
Phone: 1 (800) 839-8640

Published by AuthorHouse 02/10/2020

ISBN: 978-1-7283-4552-9 (sc)
ISBN: 978-1-7283-4551-2 (hc)
ISBN: 978-1-7283-4553-6 (e)

Library of Congress Control Number: 2020901974

Print information available on the last page.

Scripture quotations marked KJV are from the Holy Bible, King James Version (Authorized Version). First published in 1611. Quoted from the KJV Classic Reference Bible, Copyright © 1983 by The Zondervan Corporation.

This book is printed on acid-free paper.

"No one has greater love than this, that one should lay down his life for his friends"

John 15:13 DBT

CONTENTS

DEDICATION

This book is dedicated to my children; Michelle, Cristie and Warren Jr., as well as my grandchildren, Ethan, Allie, Harper and Chapman. My sincere prayer is that they never know the horrors and suffering associated with war, just as I pray no other children of the world will have to experience them either. Simultaneously, I pray all the children of the world will someday know the love of their fellow man just as the Vietnam Veterans loved one another.

Special thanks to Jessica Veltri Photography for the cover photo of the Vietnam Veterans Memorial Wall.

INTRODUCTION

J ust the sound of the word "war" instantly invokes intense emotions of death, destruction and evil. While these are natural reactions, there is another, even more powerful emotion I want you to know and understand about war. That emotion is love. Sounds ridiculous, right? I hope as you continue your journey back in time with me to the Vietnam War, you will come to understand how love ultimately manifests itself and overcomes the hate and evil associated with war.

My first edition book about the war, "Remembering Vietnam-A Veteran's Story", was a chronicle of my tour of duty in Vietnam in 1969 with the 1st Infantry Division. The original purpose of that book was to put my story into written form in order for my children and grandchildren to know my experiences, since I kept those memories hidden deep in my consciousness and I wanted them to stay there. However, with a lot of gentle encouragement from my wife, I finally found the courage to begin that journey back into the memories that kept sneaking back onto the screen of my nightly dreams. War leaves its imprint on the very soul of those who manage to survive it. Happy-go-lucky teenagers leave home and come back changed forever.

That first effort proved to be very well received by all who read it; however, I purposefully avoided relating the full truth about war or its lasting effects. I received many positive reviews and answered many inquiries about what the war was like, but I was never satisfied with my efforts. I knew I had missed the mark on what this story should be focused on.

Sometime later, I heard from a reader who challenged me with a question about one of the statements I made when I said I believed God has a plan for each life and He told me I would not die in Vietnam, but would return home to fulfill the work he planned for me. His question was, "does that mean then that God had no plan for those who were killed there?" I had not anticipated that and made a feeble attempt to explain what I meant.

That question started gnawing at me to reexamine my entire book and what exactly did the title "Remembering Vietnam" really mean and why?

Then I realized, after several decades of having an all-volunteer military and relative peace in the world, fewer and fewer Americans have any experience or association with national service. We have become complacent and lost our appreciation for the price of freedom.

Way back in antiquity, the Roman poet, Horace articulated a notion when he wrote: "Dulce et decorum est pro patria morti." (It is sweet and fitting to die for one's country". Those of us who have fought in modern wars know there is nothing sweet or fitting about it. War is brutal, evil and leaves nothing but destruction in its wake.

Elderly politicians on both sides send their very best youth to fight and die horrible deaths, often for reasons they do not understand. Most of the time there is no clear, definable goal of what "victory" is or when it is achieved. Even those who survive the brutality and evil are forever changed. Families are robbed of sons and daughters, fathers, brothers and sisters and husbands and wives for no good reason. Often when the conflict is over, nothing has changed except the death of good people while the politicians responsible pat themselves on the back, claiming some elusive victory.

By now you are probably asking yourself, where then could there be any love in the mist of such horrible holocausts?

The answer lies in the warriors themselves. These young men came from all over America with totally different educational, socio economic, political and religious differences. Yet in the chaos of combat, they soon learned they were alone to fight or die, except for the comrades with them. A comradeship and human bond developed between them that only those who served can ever begin to understand.

Most of them didn't know what this war was about or why they had to go. But go they did. They didn't hide in a closet whimpering that the cause was unjust or the price too high. When their country called, they stood up proudly and said, "take me, I'll go." They didn't mouth some lame excuse, but put their ass on the line when the chips went down. They knew the possible consequences of their actions and volunteered anyway.

That unique bond of love led these young men to the very heights of courage. No one could have predicted these seemingly ordinary young men would be capable of such heroic acts. None of them would have given up their life for all the gold in the world, yet when they saw a comrade in need, wounded or dying and pleading for help and mercy, they left the safety of their positions and plunged headlong into the maelstrom to come to the aid of a friend. Only love can explain such behavior. That love will endure in the heart of the survivors as long as they live. Love allowed them to put aside the fear for their own safety when they rushed to the aid of a friend.

Fear nor hatred or anger ever motivated men to completely disregard their own safety for that of another. Only love can do that. Evacuation crews repeatedly flew their helicopters into the thick of battle to rescue the wounded and the dead. Doctors and nurses worked around the clock in operating rooms filled with blood everywhere, young men pleading for relief from the pain of their wounds and the caregivers overwhelmed with grief as they tried to give peace and comfort to the wounded.

All 58,000 plus who died and who's names are etched on the black granite walls of their memorial in Washington, D. C., remain forever young in our memory as we are forever bound together in the arms of love for one another.

That is what is worth remembering about war, it is the warrior and how much we loved each other, what we did and who we are.

HISTORY OF VIETNAM

Modern day Vietnam emerged from the former region known as French Indochina. French influence in the region first began with the establishment of French Catholic missionaries. From 1887 until the Geneva Accord of 1954, Vietnam was a part of Indochina, a colonial possession that also included Laos and Cambodia. Even today, it is easy to find French influence throughout the region. French control brought about change to the culture that cannot now be separated, it is too deeply ingrained. Many staple foods in Vietnam are French dishes modified to include local ingredients. Much of what we know as distinctly Vietnamese cuisine has French influence. The café culture of Paris with sidewalk coffee cafes is prevalent in Vietnam today. Vietnamese tend to start their day with coffee instead of tea as preferred by other Asian cultures. Even the Vietnamese language itself was influenced. For instance, the Vietnamese words for cheese, neckties, butter, bread, father (pa), beer and many, many others are all phonetic copies of French words.

As mentioned earlier, Catholics make up approximately seven percent of the population. Holidays like Easter and Christmas, while not nearly as widely celebrated as they are in America, have their own Vietnamese traditions. It is common to see people wearing a cross around their neck, and many families have an alter to Jesus in their home, near their ancestor shrine. Also, some of the most famous buildings in Vietnam are churches such as the Notre Dame Cathedral Basilica in Saigon pictured below.

Saigon, Ho Chi Min City, is a metropolis of between 8 and nine million people with many large residential districts filled with large French style villas resembling affluent neighborhoods of Paris that were once occupied by French business tycoons and colonial political leaders.

Even the fashion world in Vietnam was influenced. While the white suits of the early 20th century are gone, there are still fashion changes evident. A traditional Vietnamese outfit, the ao dai, was more conservative prior to the French influx. It was a flowing robe which didn't accentuate the sexual parts of the body, but the French tailors helped change the traditional ao dai into what we know today as a voluptuous outfit which accentuates curves and is made of thin silk. Styles have once again changed as American influence is the norm in clothing today.

Even education was changed when the French introduced schooling of the mass public up to the third-grade level which had not been done before. Before the French, education was only for the ruling elite.

Large numbers of mixed-race children, descendants of the French and American forces occupying the country are another legacy still evident today.

The original Capital was in Saigon in 1887, then it moved to Hanoi in 1902 and back again to Saigon in 1945. After the fall of France during World War II, the colony was under Japanese occupation until March 1945. After the Japanese surrender at the end of the war, the Viet Minh, a coalition of communists and Vietnamese nationalist, led by Ho Chi Minh, declared Vietnamese Independence. The French were determined to keep control of their colony in Asia which had been very profitable for them by supplying France with cheap natural resources. Vast rubber plantations were established and tended by cheap Asian labor. The huge French tire company, Michelin, was supplied with cheap, quality rubber. The result was all out war between France and the Viet-Minh.

The Battle of Dien Bien Phu

The First Indochina War broke out in late 1946 between France and Viet Minh forces. The Viet Minh were led by Ho Chi Minh. During World War II, the United States had supported the Viet Minh in their resistance against the Japanese. Ho and his troops took to the hills and raged a guerilla war against the French occupation.

The Battle of Dien Bien Phu marked the culmination of that struggle with the defeat of French forces On May 7th, 1954. The battle began on March 13th when French forces sought to cut the Viet Minh's supply lines to Laos. To accomplish that, a large fortified base was constructed at Dien Bien Phu in Northwest Vietnam. It was their hope that the base would draw the Viet Minh into a pitched battle where superior French firepower could destroy the enemy. However, the site selected was on the low ground of the valley between mountainous terrain which the French mistakenly believed the Viet Minh could not establish artillery positions from. The Vietnamese were once again underestimated as Viet Minh forces did the unthinkable by pulling large artillery pieces up steep slopes and gaining the upper hand in firepower. They were also supplied by China and Russia with effective antiaircraft weapons which they used very effectively in limiting resupply of the French forces below from the air. As months passed with unrelenting artillery fire from above, monsoon rains and antiaircraft weapons in use by the Viet Minh, the French were cut off from all resupply of weapons, food and medical supplies. Even evacuation became impossible and the results were disastrous. In nearly two months of fighting, the entire French garrison was either killed or captured. This victory by the Viet Minh effectively ended the First Indochina War and led to the 1954 Geneva Accords which split the country into North and South Vietnam.

In order to create a political alternative to the Viet Minh, the State of Vietnam was proclaimed in 1949. On October 22nd, and November 9th, the Kingdom of Laos and Kingdom of Cambodia proclaimed their respective independence. Following the Geneva Accord of 1954, the French evacuated Vietnam and French Indochina came to an end.

The Geneva Conference on July 21st, 1954 recognized the 17th parallel north as a provisional military demarcation line, dividing the country into two zones, communist North Vietnam and pro-Western South Vietnam.

At the beginning of the First Indochina War, the United States was neutral in the conflict because of opposition in America to European colonialism. The Viet Minh had recently been our allies against the Japanese; however, the United States gradually began supporting the French in their war effort.

During the 1950s, America became concerned about the spread of Communism in Southeast Asia and President Harry Truman began covertly authorizing direct financial assistance to the French. In September 1950, President Truman sent the Military Assistance Advisory Group to Indochina to assist the French. America had been drawn into Vietnam with no awareness or concern for the consequences. President Dwight D. Eisenhower escalated American presence there in 1954 and we were committed at an ever-increasing escalation under Presidents Kennedy, Johnson and Nixon. President John Kennedy introduced some of the first overt U. S. combat forces into Vietnam.

The Indochinese people had been at war for decades in their struggle for independence. Generations of these people grew up knowing nothing but war. It was a way of life. They were determined to become a self-governing state, no matter what the costs.

American Presidents from Truman to Nixon never understood the determination of the Vietnamese people for independence. The similarities to America's own struggle for independence from colonial rule by England in the 18th century were ignored. America was committed to an unwinnable war, half a globe away in which more than 58,000 young Americans would be slaughtered. Worst of all, the American government hid the truth about America's presence there. The full truth would only surface decades later.

THE SEXY, SIZZLING SIXTIES

No story about the Vietnam War would be complete without having some background of the day and age in which it took place. The decade of the 1960s was truly remarkable for many reasons. There was racial and political unrest in America that affected every family. Violence rarely seen before was prevalent as people threw away the notion of change through peaceful means. It was the decade millions of "baby boomers" reached young adulthood following World War II. It was a new generation that had no first-hand knowledge of the life and poverty of the Great Depression or the sacrifices required of all Americans during World War II. This generation knew only peace and prosperity as a way of life.

Coming of age as a naïve, self-centered teenager at the beginning of the decade into a young man capable of shouldering immense responsibility by decade's end was a result of that most unusual decade in which I grew up. The fiery furnace of my experience in Vietnam had refined me and gave me the confidence I needed to face and master the immense tasks which lay ahead in my life. I had faced death and survived. I had seen the unspeakable evil men are capable of inflicting on one another, but I had also seen the immeasurable good that men are capable of. I learned to appreciate the things in life that really matter, like the beauty of a sunrise after a long night crouched in fear, the brightness of a full moon in a clear sky, sharing the last drop of hot, putrid water in my canteen with a thirsty friend, bathing the grime and filth off my body with the help of a gentle rain. I learned to cherish each day as if it were my last.

The 1960s began with the Presidential election in 1960 with John F. Kennedy (D) Vs Richard M. Nixon (R). For the first time in history, the new mass media platform, television, would play a major role in an election. The race was highlighted with a live Presidential debate in which the youthful Kennedy was prepared for the camera with makeup that gave him a striking appearance while the older Nixon had no makeup and looked washed out, sickly, unprepared and less energetic than his opponent. Kennedy's nomination was historic itself since he was the first Catholic to be nominated to run for President. His faith was portrayed as a liability by many as it was rumored if elected President, he would follow the decrees of the Pope in Rome, thus making the Pope an unelected U.S. President. Richard Nixon was widely known in the country after having served for eight years as Vice-President under President Dwight D. Eisenhower.

John Kennedy was relatively unknown as a young Senator representing Massachusetts. The 1960 election gave Kennedy a razor thin victory in the electoral college and only a little more than a 100,000 vote popular vote margin. Kennedy was quite inspiring though and his inaugural speech lifted an entire nation with hope and inspiration. He challenged Americans to give back to the county through their service, either in the military or through government programs such as the Peace Corps. He also set a very ambitious goal for the country to land a man on the moon by the end of the decade. That goal seemed to cement the country together working toward a common goal. Many said it could not be done in that short time span, but it was accomplished in 1969 with astronaut Neil Armstrong being the first human to set foot on the moon.

Kennedy's election marked the beginning of much social and political unrest in the country. Soon after taking the reins of leadership, his young administration was challenged by the Soviet Union with their intrusion into Cuba, only 90 miles south of Key West, Florida. Their threat of a nuclear presence so close to our border could not be left unchallenged. The confrontation of the world's only nuclear powers that followed came very close to a disastrous nuclear holocaust, but Kennedy stood strong and forced the Russians to back down and withdraw.

Socially, several watershed movements took place during the decade with the introduction of the American Civil Rights movement, the feminist movement, the beginning of the environmental movement, the drug culture and gay liberation.

Activist Dr. Martin Luther King, Jr., spearheaded the Civil Rights movement in which he advocated peaceful demonstration as a means to call attention to the cause. Other organizations soon joined that movement including the Black Panther Party and the rise of Black Power. The latter organizations however, advocated violence and destruction as a method to achieve their stated goals.

The feminist movement questioned for the first time the long-held belief that the woman's place was in the home and the family was more important than the individual. New forms of birth control were introduced that resulted in a dramatic change in women's sexual behavior, no longer having to worry about unwanted pregnancies. Notions of pre-marital sex changed drasticaly and the decade was characterized with the slogan, "Make love, not War". It was a real sexual revolution in which Hugh Hefner's Playboy Magazine came of age in America.

The decade also experienced the widespread use of marijuana and psychedelic drugs such as LSD. The new drug culture meshed perfectly with the feminist movement and "Love Ins" were popular throughout the country. One popular song of the time had a line that went like this, "When you can't be with the one you love honey, love the one you're with." Professor Timothy Leary from California was the most notable of the drug culture with his advocation of LSD.

Even the music of the decade was changed with a new emphasis of rebellion against authority. The old AM radio stations with only a limited broadcast range were replaced with the new technology of FM radio that reached a much wider audience. Hard Rock music found its beginnings in the decade that included the following musical groups: The Grateful Dead, Pink Floyd, Jimi Hendrix, The Byrds, Janice Joplin, Crosby, Stills and Nash, The Doors, Country Joe and the Fish, Big Brother and Jefferson Airplane. Scott McKenzie's rendition of the song, "If you're going to San Francisco" became a world-wide hit. American GIs adopted it as their theme song and associated it with their trip "back to the world" after serving their tours in Vietnam.

Women, minorities and college students weren't the only people demanding change. Even the farm community joined in with the formation of the NFO, National Farm Organization that sought to organize the farm community to improve commodity prices by withholding food products from the economy to improve the prices for their products. Several violent incidents occurred as a result of their demonstrations.

Key figures of the decade include: Muhammad Ali, Saul Alinski, Bill Ayers, Bernardine Dorn, Bob Dylan, Daniel Ellsberg, Jane Fonda, and Jerry Garcia, just to name a few.

Political unrest was prevalent around the globe during this decade and was not confined to the United States. There were violent protests in France, The Troubles in Northern Ireland, Mexico City and guerilla warfare in Brazil. The Six Day War occurred from June 5th thru June 10th,1967 in the Middle East when Israel initiated a very successful preemptive strike against Egypt, Jordan and Syria. Israeli soldiers captured and occupied the Sinai Peninsula, the West Bank, The Gaza Strip, East Jerusalem and the Golan Heights. The Holy City of Jerusalem was reunited for the first time in many years.

Earlier in the decade, President Kennedy authorized and introduced an escalation of American forces into Vietnam, known more commonly as Indochina.

The very popular President Kennedy was assassinated on November 22, 1963 while visiting Dallas, Texas. That event temporarily froze the nation as Vice-President Lyndon B. Johnson was sworn in as President.

President Johnson, in concert with Defense Secretary Robert McNamara, oversaw a dramatic new escalation of the war in Vietnam. Secretary McNamara convinced the President his new tactics for waging war would bring a quick and easy military victory. Neither would take place. There was no clear cause for our intrusion, no clear plan for waging the war nor was there a clearly articulated goal as to what constituted victory. Neither military nor political leaders understood the will of the enemy to win and keep independence at any cost. With each new challenge militarily in Vietnam, President Johnson responded with the introduction of more troops. At the peak of deployment, more than 500,000 servicemen and women were "in country" Vietnam for the war effort. Traditional military recruitment could not produce the numbers required to meet the President's goals and the system of conscription, known as the Selective Service System was instituted. The system was flawed in many ways, especially in the beginning, with exemptions for various groups that tended to be the upper middle class and upper-class young men, resulting in the conscription of lower socio-economic young Americans bearing the greatest burden. McNamara was convinced his strategy of overwhelming force resulting in high enemy death rates would force the enemy into submission. McNamara did not understand the enemy he faced. Fatality rates meant nothing to them. Ho Chi Minh stated we could kill ten of them while suffering only one loss of our own, and they would win the war. Ho realized what Johnson did not, that with enough casualties, America would lose its will to fight a war the people did not understand.

The Tet Offensive of 1968 saw the North Vietnamese forces attack more than 100 cities in the south in large numbers. The strike was a total surprise to American troops and marked the turning point in American opinion against the war.

College campuses experienced violent demonstrations against the war all across the country. Many left-wing groups took root such as the Students for a Democratic Society. A more virulent offshoot, The Weather Underground, headed by a young militant activist, Bill Ayers, along with Bernardine Dorn led with violence and bombings throughout the country in protest against the war. Military recruitment centers and even the Pentagon itself were targets. The near disaster of the bloody battle of Khe Sanh during the tet offensive of 1968 also helped fuel the anti-war sentiment. That sentiment centered not only on the politicians directing it, but on the American GIs fighting in it. The American soldier, for the first time, was looked upon as a co-conspirator and war criminal by many in the country. Ayers and Dorn were wanted by the FBI in connection with the bombings of government buildings and they went into hiding. They eventually surfaced, were arrested and charges of domestic terrorism were brought against them. The charges were eventually dropped when it was learned the FBI had gathered evidence against them without first obtaining proper warrants. Ayers and Dorn went on to become Professors at the University of Chicago. Ayers became a political advisor to Chicago Mayor Richard Daley and later helped introduce another young street activist, Barack Obama to the political scene.

Dr. Martin Luther King, Jr. was assassinated April 4th, 1968 and President John Kennedy's brother Robert fell to an assassin's bullet on June 5th, 1968 while campaigning for the Presidential election of 1968. Dr. King's death brought violent protests across America following The Long Hot Summer of 1967 when there were 159 race riots in Atlanta, Boston,

Cincinnati, Buffalo, Tampa, New York City, Minneapolis and Rochester. Anarchy was the rule of the day.

The Democratic Convention met in 1968 in Chicago to nominate their party's representative in the fall Presidential election. The convention was nearly cancelled due to violent protests throughout the city in opposition to the war in Vietnam. The Democrat Party had become the symbol of the unpopular war. The Chicago Police met the protestors with strong defensive tactics and eventually had to enlist the help of the National Guard in order to maintain law and order. Television spread first-hand video of the chaos and destruction both in Chicago and throughout the country.

Early on, prior to the Chicago convention, President Lyndon Johnson threw the Democrat Party into chaos when he announced he would not accept their nomination to run for President and if nominated, he would not take part, and if elected, would not serve. The weight of the tragedy he had overseen in Vietnam and the responsibility he bore for sending hundreds of thousands of American youth to Vietnam and the subsequent deaths of more than 58,000 had taken its toll. Their blood was on his hands. President Johnson never recovered from the nightmare he had overseen.

The Democrat Party nominated a very weak candidate, Hubert H. Humphrey in Johnson's place. The once defeated Richard Nixon made a resurgence and captured the Republican nomination and subsequently ran on the promise of bringing the war in Vietnam to an end and he was elected overwhelmingly for that purpose.

THE PENTAGON PAPERS

THE TRUTH BEGINS TO SURFACE

Secretary of Defense, Robert McNamara created "The Vietnam Study Task Force" on June 17th, 1967 for the stated purpose of writing an encyclopedic history of the Vietnam War. Whatever his purpose for the Task Force was, McNamara failed to inform either President Lyndon Johnson or Secretary of State Dean Rusk.

The findings of the study were compiled by thirty-six analyst, half of them active duty military officers and the rest were academics and civilian federal employees. In order to keep the study secret from others, including National Security Advisor Walt W. Rostow, they conducted no interviews or consultations with the armed forces, with the White house, or with other federal agencies.

McNamara left the Defense Department in February 1968 and the finished study was presented to his successor, Clark M. Clifford, who claimed he never read it. The study consisted of 3,000 pages of historical analysis and 4,000 pages of original government documents that had been classified "Top Secret and Sensitive".

The report revealed many stunning revelations about America's involvement in Southeast Asia that had been kept secret from the American public. In 1950 under the direction of President Harry S. Truman, the United States provided large scale military equipment to the French in their war against the Viet Minh in order to maintain their colonial rule in Vietnam. In 1954, the United States began to engage in "acts of sabotage and terror warfare" in defense of South Vietnam against communist North Vietnam. In 1955, the United States encouraged and directly assisted South

Vietnamese President Ngo Dinh Diem's rise to power. In 1963, under President John F. Kennedy, the United States encouraged and directly assisted the overthrow of the South Vietnamese President Ngo Dinh Diem. On August 2, 1964, President Lyndon B. Johnson manipulated public opinion following the Gulf of Tonkin Incident in preparation for open warfare against a communist takeover of South Vietnam.

Although President Johnson claimed the aim of the Vietnam War was to secure an "independent, non-communist South Vietnam", a January 1965 memorandum by Secretary of Defense Robert McNamara stated that an underlying justification was not to help a friend, but to contain China. McNamara sent another memorandum to President Johnson on November 3rd, 1965 in which he explained the major policy decisions with respect to our course of action in Vietnam. The memo stated the decision to bomb North Vietnam and the July 1965 approval of Phase 1 deployments made sense only if they were in support of a long-run United States policy to contain China. McNamara convinced Johnson America must contain China to prevent them from organizing all of Asia in opposition to the United States. His plan entailed establishment of three fronts against China. First was the Japan-Korean front, next was the India-Pakistan front and finally the Southeast Asia front.

On August 2, 1964, the destroyer USS Maddox was performing a signals intelligence patrol off the coast of North Vietnam when they were approached by North Vietnamese torpedo boats. The Maddox initiated the incident by firing three warning shots and the North Vietnamese responded with torpedoes and machine gun fire. A brief naval battle followed in which 3 North Vietnamese boats were damaged, 4 North Vietnamese sailors were killed while the Maddox was unscathed.

It was originally claimed that a second Gulf of Tonkin incident occurred on August 4th, 1964, but this claim was later proven to be false. The out-come however, was passage by the United States Congress of the Gulf of Tonkin Resolution which granted President Johnson the authority to assist any Southeast Asian country whose government was considered to be jeopardized by "communist aggression". The resolution served as Johnson's legal justification for deploying U. S. conventional forces and the commencement of open warfare against North Vietnam.

The American people had been intentionally deceived into believing a threat to our national security was at stake. No such risk existed, yet more than 58,000 of America's finest youth would be sent there to die for a non-existent threat.

In June 1971, The New York Times began publishing excerpts of the secret documents that had been leaked to them by Daniel Ellsberg. Ellsberg had worked on the task force and had access to all its conclusions. The Time's publication of these classified documents set off a firestorm against them and against Ellsberg. The government sought to suppress further publication by The Times, but the Supreme Court held forth a momentous decision upholding the 1st amendment rights of a free press. The government also brought charges of espionage and other crimes against Ellsberg, but they too were later dismissed.

The truth about the war and America's involvement was finally out. The anti-war movement in America felt justified in their belief this had been an illegal war and that the government and the country's military were war criminals and guilty of genocide. In light of these facts, it is no wonder American GIs were treated with disrespect and dishonor upon their return. They had survived the horrors of war in the jungles of Vietnam only to be confronted with another enemy when they returned.

WARREN ROBINSON

THE MY LAI MASSACRE

Adding more fuel to the fire of sentiment against the military was the My Lai massacre which occurred March 16th, 1968; however it was not made public until November, 1969. This gruesome and heinous incident of the war further cemented a public outcry around the globe for an end to the war.

The massacre resulted in the deaths of between 347 and 504 civilians including men, women, children and infants by U. S. troops. Some of the women were gang raped and their bodies mutilated as were children as young as 12. The massacre was perpetrated by twenty-six soldiers of Company C, 1st Battalion, 20th Infantry Regiment and Company B, 4th Battalion, 3rd Infantry Regiment, 11th Brigade, 23rd (Americal) Infantry Division. Lieutenant William Calley, Jr., a platoon leader in C Company was the only soldier convicted. He was found guilty of killing 22 villagers and was originally given a life sentence, but served only three and a half years under house arrest. The incident occurred in two hamlets, My Lai and My Khe in Quang Ngai Province.

When the scope of the killing and cover-up attempts were exposed, three servicemen who had tried to halt the massacre and rescue the hiding civilians were shunned and even denounced as traitors by several U. S. Congressmen. Thirty year later, they were recognized and decorated, one posthumously, by the U. S. Army for shielding non-combatants from harm in a war zone. My Lai, along with the Gun Ri massacre in South Korea were the largest publicized massacres of civilians by U. S. forces in the 20th century.

Charlie Company, 1st Battalion, 20th Infantry Regiment, 11th Brigade, 23rd Infantry Division arrived in South Vietnam in December 1967. Their first three months in country passed without direct contact with North Vietnamese-backed forces. By mid-March of 1968 however, they had suffered 28 casualties involving mines or booby-traps and two days before the massacre, the company lost a popular sergeant to a land mine.

During the 1968 Tet Offensive, U. S. intelligence believed the Viet Cong 48th Local Force Battalion was taking refuge in villages in the area and that the civilians were giving them sanctuary. U. S. forces had previously tried to secure the villages in the area from the Viet Cong with only limited success.

On March 16th through the 18th, the decision was made to engage the enemy in the area and to destroy the remnants of the VC 48th Battalion. Before the operation began, Colonel Oran K. Henderson, the 11th Brigade commander, urged his officers to "go in there aggressively, close with the enemy and wipe them out for good". In turn, Lieutenant Colonel Barker reportedly ordered the 1st Battalion commanders to burn the houses, kill the livestock, destroy food supplies and destroy the wells.

On the eve of the attack, at a Charlie Company briefing, Captain Ernest Medina told his men that nearly all the civilian residents of the villages would have left for the market by 7:00 AM, and that any who remained would be Viet Cong or Viet Cong sympathizers. He was asked if the order included the killing of women and children. The troops present at the briefing gave different accounts of his reply. He was quoted as saying, "They're all VC, now go and get them", and was heard to reply to the question "Who is my enemy?", by saying, "Anybody that was running from us, hiding from us, or appeared to be the enemy. If a man was running, shoot him, sometimes even if a woman was running, shoot her."

At Calley's trial, one defense witness testified that he remembered Medina instructing them to destroy everything in the village that was "walking, crawling or growing".

While flying over the village of Song My, providing close air support for ground forces, Warrant Officer Hugh Thompson, Jr., a helicopter pilot saw dead and wounded civilians. He landed his helicopter near a ditch that was full of dead bodies but there was also some movement. Thompson asked a sergeant he encountered there to help get the people out of the ditch, and the sergeant replied he would help get them out of their misery. Thompson, shocked and confused, then spoke with Calley, who claimed to be just following orders.

Thompson then loaded as many survivors as possible onto his helicopter, flew them to safety and reported what he had witnessed. His actions finally led to an end of the massacre and he was awarded the Distinguished Flying Cross.

War is such an evil force, it can consume even good men and lead them to commit horrible crimes like these. There is no excuse for this behavior and the massacre marks a truly despicable event of the war.

MY STORY

THE JOURNEY BEGINS

Military medals are awarded for many reasons. The Medal of Honor is awarded for "Heroism above and beyond the ordinary call of duty". The Purple Heart is awarded to servicemen and women who are wounded by an enemy force while serving in an active combat zone. I was awarded two Bronze Star Medals and one Army Commendation Medal, but the one medal regarded lest by most people is the National Defense Service Medal, which every service member is awarded when they enter military service. In my opinion, this medal is perhaps the greatest of all. This medal signifies that person was willing to step forward and write their country a blank check, payable with their very life if necessary.

The bravest men I ever knew were the combat medics, helicopter "dust off" crews, and helicopter door gunners.

The medics would rush into an active combat kill zone, ignoring the danger to themselves, armed with nothing more than a simple medical kit, in an attempt to save the life of a fellow comrade. The dust-off crews would routinely fly into the thick of an active fire fight, knowing they were sitting ducks for enemy fire to pick up wounded GIs that needed to be rushed to an emergency hospital. The average life span of a door-gunner was only six months, yet man after man would volunteer for it since somebody had to do it.

Many men refused to take part in the Vietnam War. They had many excuses, including they considered the war to be unjust or they did not believe in taking up arms to kill another person, etc. Some fled illegally to Canada for refuge, some sought exemptions in other ways, but most were just cowards who wanted someone else to risk dying in their place. I confess to harboring anger and ill will in my heart for these men for more than fifty years. I also confess it has been very difficult to accept the decision made by President Jimmy Carter to issue a blanket pardon for those who fled to Canada while others were forced to take their place, then allowed to return home as if nothing ever happened and enjoy the fruits of America's freedom and wealth. However, I have recently been able to let those feeling go, realizing it was only eating away at me, not them. By doing that I have come to know a peace I have never experienced before. I feel nothing for these men now but pity. I pity them for never experiencing the love and comradeship the rest of us had that remains as strong as it ever did and will continue until the last one moves on to heaven and hears a hearty, "Welcome Home Brother!" I pity them for never being able to feel the pride we have, and finally, many decades later, the respect and honor America has shown us. They will never be able to tell their grandchildren how they chose to stand with their fellow men, and how they experienced a love they will never forget. This narrative is to honor all those ordinary young men and women who served with pride and honor but received no thanks or recognition other than the National Defense Service Medal for putting their very lives at risk.

With the tumultuous history of the 1960s as a backdrop, I begin the story of my own journey to, through and home again from Vietnam in 1969. I hope the reader will obtain a little better understanding of the lives and emotions these young men experienced during those most trying times, including the dramatic change their experience made in their lives then and for every moment since. Hundreds of books have been written and published about the Vietnam experience, describing the gory details of horrific battles large and small, the brutality and sheer evil that raged rampant, but this book strives to relate the way those experiences changed their very souls, along with the greatest force in the universe, love for one's fellow man as Jesus instructed us. Look for that theme throughout the book. This account also relates my personal story of how God has intervened in my life in unexpected ways and times to steer me back onto the path he set out for me for the advancement of his kingdom. Many other veterans have related their similar experiences with God while serving in Vietnam.

Looking back 50 years ago, we still don't quite understand what that war was all about. It was one of the few times in American history, with the exception of the Pacific Theatre in World II, where we fought a determined guerilla enemy in his own back yard. The terrain of Vietnam lent itself perfectly to this type of warfare and was very successful. This was the enemy's back yard where he knew every secret of the terrain. The enemy was determined, smart, resourceful and could strike, then melt back into the jungle as if they were ghosts.

By day, they were ordinary looking Vietnamese doing ordinary tasks. The girl pictured above may have been a "hooch girl", cleaning hoochies on a military installation by day, fighting GIs by night. They were farmers, barbers, cooks and were around you every day, only to surface at night to carry out their clandestine activities. The only other time in our nation's history we were involved in such warfare on a large scale was the Revolutionary War and America was the guerilla force then that defeated the mightiest military in the world at that time, Great Britain. Washington, DC politicians directed this political war, refusing to let the military do their job, a mistake we never seem to learn from.

DECISION TIME

After graduation from High School in 1963, I began to hear more and more news stories about a seemingly unimportant little country on the other side of the world with a strange name, Vietnam. I had to locate it on a world map in order to know where it was. It looked so tiny then and seemingly unimportant, why was it worth all the concern to America, I wondered. I vaguely remembered reading about the connection it had with France and how the communists had driven them out. President Kennedy had even sent a few American military "advisors" there. It was of no concern to me then and I believed it would simply fade into history. I went on to Georgia Tech for two years and graduated from Valdosta State University at the head of my graduating class in 1967. I was ready to set the world on fire with my enthusiasm, believing I "knew it all". I was so confident I would complete undergrad school with a degree in some field related to finance, then a law degree, and I was destined for some prestigious position in a high paying job in the city. Little did I know, God had other plans for my future. His plan would take me on a very different path in life. His plan involved bringing me back down to earth, humble me and make me realize how blessed I was for the many privileges I enjoyed each day that I had only taken for granted before. It would take many decades for me to realize, I was destined for His work on earth and not my own.

It was becoming more evident that the tiny nuisance halfway around the world was steadily escalating into a full-blown war. Why had America become involved, I wondered? U.S. casualties continued to mount every month and as they increased, it became very unpopular and soon divided the nation politically. As casualty reports were announced every day, it became necessary to institute the draft system again in order to continue fueling the war machine America had now become. Chet Huntley, David Brinkley and Walter Cronkite hosted popular nightly newscasts on TV that showed for the first time in history, current video of this very nasty guerilla war that America never seemed to have a will to fight or a plan to win. Popular opinion in America against the war continued to increase and politicians were beginning to push for an exit from the war. We all watched intently every night, because these were the only TV news casts each day, since 24-hour news channels would not be conceived for more than a decade later. The average week's report of the number killed in action during that time was 289 per week. In addition to the nightly news stories of the war, newspapers and magazines throughout the country headlined the stories of all the young men killed that week. The decision to volunteer for service during this time was truly a sobering and frightening one for millions of young Americans.

Before graduation from College, I began to formulate plans for my future, and I decided I wanted to study the law, then move on to bigger and better things. I had no intention or desire to ever return home to Lenox, Georgia and be a part of the business my grandfather started in 1906, The Bank of Lenox. My father replaced his father as owner and head of the bank in 1941 and I assumed he would be around for many years to come since he was a young 56 years old. I applied to Mercer University Law School, Emory University Law School and The University of Georgia Law School and received acceptances for admission to all three. I sought the advice of a family friend, Judge H. W. Lott, as to which one he would advise me to attend and he recommended The University of Georgia. He explained that at the University, I would come into contact with many more young attorneys who would be located throughout the state. Those contacts would become very valuable in the future. The summer of 1967 rapidly passed and before the end of August, I loaded my car with meager belongings and began the trip North to Athens on the new interstate highway through Lenox, I-75. Somewhere between Lenox and Tifton, the thought occurred to me from out of nowhere, what if I go to law school and get drafted into military service? I had not seriously considered this outcome before and I exited the highway, turned around and drove South to Adel to pay a visit to my local draft board about this possibility. The draft office was located in the basement of the old Adel Post Office building and was run by a kindly looking old white-haired lady named Miss Minnie Shaw. Miss Minnie listened patiently to my story, never once giving any indication there would be bad news to my inquiry. When I finished, she looked me in the eyes and said without hesitation in her sweet kindly voice, "Warren, if you go to graduate school, you will most likely receive a draft notice within a few months." The words from her mouth stunned me because I had not even considered this outcome before.

I left Adel, returned home with my car still packed and broke the news to my parents. For the next few days I struggled with the question of what to do next. I knew my dad had spent a lot of money on my education up to that date with two years at Darlington School, a private college preparatory school in Rome, Ga. Then four more years of College and there would be even more expense to pay for Law School. I appreciated what my parents had sacrificed for me up to that point, and I soon decided it would not be fair to ask them to do more without the prospect I would be able to complete the course. I knew I needed a little time to sort things out. I also knew that teachers in the fields of math and science were exempted from the draft, so I visited Mr. Herschel Sessions, Superintendent of Cook County Schools to inquire about the possibility of being hired as a teacher in the Cook County School System. Mr. Sessions seemed delighted to hear from me and said the new fall session was about to begin and he had been unable to fill the position of 8th grade math teacher at Cook County High School. He immediately offered me the job with a one-year contract at the astounding salary of $400.00 per month! I accepted the offer with the understanding I would begin taking courses in Education at Valdosta State University in order to be licensed to teach on a provisional permit, which I did. I moved into an apartment in Adel and began supporting myself for the first time while I sorted my future out without having the threat of being drafted hanging over me. It was a rather lonely existence but it was perfect to sort out my future.

I rather enjoyed the experience of teaching 8th grade math and watch the kids, not much younger than I, begin to grasp the basics of a world of mathematics beyond just the one plus one equals two level they were accustomed to. I was told by the Principal and older teachers there I was doing a good job, my students reported that I was very strict with discipline and I did not grade them on the curve, which they had been accustomed to. I gave each one the grade they earned. If they wanted a good grade, they had to actually work for it. However, it took me only a few months to realize this was not a satisfactory solution to my dilemma. More and more I listened to the news accounts at night about the war and I soon felt very guilty, knowing that because I found an exemption from the draft, some other young American would have to take my place there and I decided I would finish my obligation to the school system, join the Army and take my medicine, whatever that might be. I knew it would be an unpopular decision, but I knew it was the right one for me. My decision came during the heaviest fighting of the war. I do not claim to be a brave man, but I knew I was not a coward. I never even entertained the notion of not serving my country when it needed me. It is said a coward dies a thousand deaths, but a brave man only dies once. Before the end of my contract, I informed Mr. Sessions of my decision so he would have plenty of time to find a replacement. After the 1967-1968 session ended in late May, I returned for another visit with Miss Minnie and told her I was ready to take my place, but I wanted to volunteer for the draft, go to the head of the list, knowing I was volunteering for Vietnam but my military obligation would be finished in two years. She accommodated me and I received my draft notice within two weeks. I never told my parents, leaving them to believe Miss Shaw had somehow done that to me. I regret never telling them the truth because they had hard feelings about her that were unwarranted. Today, I cannot imagine the stress Miss Minnie experienced by having to send young Cook County boys, many she had known since birth, into combat. They would leave almost weekly on one of those Greyhound busses, and some would never return. In a small community like ours, everybody knew everybody else and the pressure must have been overwhelming.

BASIC TRAINING

The draft notice read something like this: "Greetings from the President of the United States of America. You are hereby ordered to report to your local draft office on the date specified herein by 9:00 AM. Bring enough clothing and personal items to last 7 days and enough money to purchase incidental items for up to a month". It was clear there was no turning back. I reported as instructed, alone, received my paperwork from Miss Minnie and stepped outside into the hot summer of South Georgia to wait with all the other Cook County boys for the Greyhound Bus to stop and begin our journey to face an uncertain future in an unknown land. The bus soon arrived and we filed on board, bound for induction processing at the Naval Air Station in Jacksonville, Florida. I am sure there were many on that bus who had never been away from home, let alone as far away as Jacksonville. We arrived later that day, checked in and received instructions on what would happen next. Military "chit" slips were issued to everyone that entitled us to one evening meal and one breakfast at the S&S cafeteria in downtown Jacksonville, along with one other, good for one night's stay at a local downtown hotel, double occupancy required. The military rented most of the downtown hotels specifically for this purpose. The City of Jacksonville looked as if it had been invaded with thousands of young men roaming the streets, ready to have one last "night on the town." Downtown was packed with bars, eager to give the boys what they wanted, never even asking for IDs, eagerly serving scores of underage boys who would become men in just a few months when they arrived in Vietnam. Many of those boys were trying alcohol for the first time. With raging hormones, these boys were served by scantily clad young ladies, some dancing on the tables, others willing and ready to give them what they wanted most, for an agreed upon fee, of course.

Military buses picked us up in front of our hotels the next morning and we were taken to the induction center for processing, a procedure that would take a few days to complete. I remember one tall, lanky boy from Kentucky I believe, who was just ahead of me in the processing line and required very thick glasses to get around. Sometimes we would have to take him by his shoulder to guide him to the next stop. At each station along the way, he would show the person in charge a letter from his doctor stating he was declared legally blind, along with a copy of his latest income tax return where he claimed the exemption for the blind. He protested he could not be required to perform military service and each time he was passed on to the next station. At the last station, his paperwork was stamped in big, bold red text which read, "Qualified for service worldwide". The last time I saw him was at the swearing-in ceremony and he had been officially inducted, available for service anywhere in the world. I have often wondered what happened to him after that. The officer in charge marched us outside and instructed us to form up in rows for the induction. Most of us remained silent, even though we had been told to repeat the oath after him. Afterward, the officer said to take one step forward if we accepted the oath and as if in one last gasp for freedom, we all took one step backward. The officer never seemed to notice and immediately welcomed us into the military service of the United States.

I will never forget what happened next as a group of men who called themselves Gideons, came to each of us, shook our hand and handed us a small New Testament of God's Holy Word as they prayed for each man. I tucked mine inside my shirt pocket and there it would remain for all the journey thereafter, even thru the "Valley of the Shadow of Death". That little Testament occupies a place of honor in my office to this day.

I believed we had all been inducted for service with the Army, but much to my surprise that was not necessarily the case. The war in Vietnam had become a "meat grinder" and all the branches were desperately in need of fresh meat, us. We filled a large airport hangar and were instructed to count off from one to 500. I was number 498. We were told we had been selected to serve in the Army. The next 500 were inducted into the Marines, the next group into the Airforce and then the Navy. I missed being a Marine by 3 men! Whew!

Later that day, we boarded airplanes at the Naval Air Station and were soon airborne, with no idea of our destination. Many guys had never flown before and it was at first an exciting adventure for them, but that was not for long. We flew for several hours in what I believed to be a Westerly direction. Shortly after dark, we landed at another Air Force Base, deplaned and I asked an airman on the ground where we were. He said you are in the State of Mississippi and you are most likely headed for Fort Polk, Louisiana. After a long bus ride through what at night seemed to be hundreds of miles of desolate countryside, his assumption was confirmed with our arrival just before dawn at Fort Polk, Louisiana for basic training.

As we lined up in ranks for our "welcome instructions", I noticed how diverse the group was and it was easy to make judgments about people's backgrounds. Many had long hair, were poorly dressed, poorly educated, others with neat haircuts, properly dressed and obviously from very different backgrounds. Many young men were here because they had been in trouble with the law and a judge had given them the choice of going to jail or volunteering for military service. Some thought they were headed for an exciting adventure in an exotic land, some just wanted to get away from a bad home life, but no one could ever fully understand what lay ahead.

Fort Polk was located near a small West Louisiana military town called Leesville. Downtown Leesville consisted mainly of about 15 or 20 bars lining both sides of the downtown street, one bank, one church and a Greyhound Bus Station. Saturday night in Leesville reminded me of Dodge City Kansas in a popular TV series at the time called "Gunsmoke" starring James Arness as Sheriff Matt Dillon. Fort Polk was a typical army base at the time and all the facilities were leftover remnants from World War II. The barracks could best be described as a fire trap. It was hard to believe this would be "home" for the next six weeks. Even the Army considered it a fire trap. A list was made up of all the names in the barracks and each night, two or three men were assigned to patrol the two-story building, walking the halls and stairway to wake up the others if a fire was detected during the night. As he completed his time slot, he would locate the next name on the list and awaken the replacement during the middle of the night. The replacement was instructed to put on his boots and helmet, grab a flashlight and begin the next round, all the while continuing to patrol in his underwear.

During the next few days all those differences would disappear with everybody getting a "GI" haircut, new olive-green uniforms that never fit and two pairs of shiny new boots that often didn't fit either. The first step had been made to turn this group of "civilians" into a homogenous team. The Army had a very effective method of removing individuality and replacing it with uniform, disciplined behavior of obeying orders without question, even to the point of what amounted to suicide instructions. Physical exhaustion, sleep deprivation and overwhelming hunger will change behavior patterns rapidly. The first few days consisted of being issued uniforms, boots, "dog tags" that identified each man's name, his social security number and his service number along with his blood type and religious preference. The purpose being to help identify the wearer if killed in combat and unrecognizable. Before training began, we were assigned tasks just to keep us busy and occupied. Once, I was assigned a pickax and told to join that day's lawn maintenance crew. Our task was to walk as a group and swing the pick into the ground making a small hole and thereby "aerating" the grass. After a long day aerating the dirt, during the intense heat of southern Louisiana in the middle of June, physical endurance increased rapidly. The training was intense with very few breaks and lots of physical training, sleep deprivation and instilling the reaction to respond immediately to barked orders without question, no matter what the command might be. Another day, we were instructed to fill thousands of sandbags and build a small dam in a little creek near our barracks. At the end of the day, we were exhausted, but very proud of the little pond our efforts had built. Much to our surprise, we were up and working again by five AM with instructions to tear it all down again so the next group of incoming troops would build it back.

A typical day began at 5:00 o'clock in the morning with a loud Drill Sargent banging on the metal lid of a trash can. Next, we dressed in our fatigue uniforms and boots, made up our bed so that it was perfect and would bounce a quarter when tossed on it. These basic tasks had to be completed very quickly, then form up outside where the DI would inspect our boots and the brass on our belt buckles. If they were not shined properly, you were disciplined. Then the morning physical training session began with a strenuous training session followed by a long run in formation around the long block, all before breakfast and sunrise. More training was worked into the day by making each trainee stand at attention in line and traverse monkey bars to enter the mess hall. If you failed to complete this task, you made your way to the end of the line and began the test again until you completed it successfully before being allowed into the mess hall. Once into the mess hall and seated for breakfast, you had only about five minutes before being forced to exit. As a result, everybody literally inhaled their food. Then, the day's training with only a few breaks began.

The first Sunday we were allowed to go to the PX to purchase necessities and just hang out for a while. Out back was a covered patio area where everybody was drinking cheap beer and listening to a jukebox with one popular song playing over and over, Johnny Cash singing "Folsom Prison Blues." Guys joked that Folsom Prison would be a step up from Ft. Polk.

A few days after settling into our new "home", one of our Drill Sergeants decided the grounds around our barracks needed "sprucing up a little". A sneaky looking recruit was selected as the platoon's one man "procurement detail" and was authorized to "procure" shrubbery using the cover of darkness. Many mornings we would go outside and notice freshly planted shrubbery that eventually stretched around the entire building. Simultaneously, shrubbery mysteriously disappeared from spots all around the base, including some from the chapel itself.

One basic training duty universally detested by all recruits was (KP), kitchen police duty. For us it would begin around 3:00 AM with a rude awakening and the order to report for KP duty. The mess hall sergeant was a "little Caesar" and he made it clear you were trespassing in his "kingdom". My first duty usually was to take stacks of dirty pots outside and clean them the hard way, with steel wool, comet cleanser and lots of elbow grease. There seemed to be an endless supply of dirty pots to clean no matter how many I brought back inside. If, by chance, Caesar saw you had nothing left to clean, he made sure you had a huge sack of potatoes to wash and peel. At lunch, I was on the serving line to dish out generous portions of some culinary "masterpiece" or another. It was made perfectly clear that if you asked for a particular serving, you better be prepared to clean your plate, leftovers were frowned upon. One time I was assigned to the receiving window to take the dirty plates and scrap the contents into a huge barrel. I had to be careful not to let anything like paper napkins or such into the mix since the remains, "slop", were picked up by a local farmer to be fed to his hogs. Caesar would occasionally make me take both hands and plunge them up to my elbows in slop and stir up the contents to prove the purity. I never saw the pigs, but I'm certain they must have heartily approved.

One activity that required a lot of time was training in the use of the M14 assault rifle. The army had developed a very effective method of training raw recruits with no prior experience in the use of weapons of any kind. Every recruit soon learned to be very competent marksmen. Within a few days of training, we could take the weapon completely apart and put it back together within a few minutes, a skill that could save your life in a combat situation even during the monsoon rains of Vietnam at night. We trained exclusively with M14 rifles, leftovers from a couple of decades before, instead of the latest ones in use in Vietnam, the Colt M16. The M16 weapon was much lighter and more easily carried all day through the hostile environment of the jungles; however, the first ones issued had many problems the army had not anticipated, such as the rifle's tendency to jam and required frequent cleanings in an environment of jungles and frequent river crossings. Another problem with the ammunition was also later identified. This rifle had been rushed into use in Vietnam without proper testing of the rifle and ammunition it fired. It was detested by the troops in the field, because their lives were at stake, armed with a weapon that was not dependable. The first time I ever fired the weapon used in Vietnam, the M16, was a few days before I left the states. My preparation for Vietnam service consisted of three days training at Homestead Air Force Base, Florida. We were given brief instruction on the M-16 assault rifle and I was allowed to actually fire one magazine of ammunition. Later, we did a mock ambush procedure that was just plain dumb. By the time I arrived in Vietnam, the rifle and ammunition had been greatly improved to eliminate many of the prior problems. However, it was still inferior to the enemy assault weapon, the AK47. The AK was heavier and more difficult to carry for long periods in the jungles but was more dependable, in contrast with the M16. The AK47 was almost indestructible in the same environment with deadly kill power. I grew up doing a lot of hunting and was very familiar with guns. As a result, I was a good marksman, and before long I was one of the best marksmen in my training group, being awarded the "Expert Marksman" badge. I remember one night when our DI, drill instructor, came through the barracks and asked a recruit if he had cleaned his weapon thoroughly that afternoon, to which the recruit replied that he had indeed cleaned his "gun". The DI screamed that we were never to call a rifle a "gun" and that we were going to now learn the difference. We were ordered to get our rifles, strip to our underwear, put on our boots and assemble outside in formation. For a least the next hour we marched around the barracks carrying our rifle on the right shoulder with the right hand, singing a cadence song, "This is my rifle", then grasping our groin with the left hand and singing," this is my gun, one is for fighting and one is for fun."

The rifle training range was a grueling ten-mile march in formation from our company area and was exhausting in the hot, humid July Louisiana sun. As with most marches, cadences were sung and were very helpful in keeping everybody in step and were often amusing as they kept our minds off our other problems. While marching, the drill instructor would sing out in a loud voice a lyric, then we would repeat it after him. The lyrics were changed often so they did not become boring. One cadence I remember went like this ", Ain't no use in looking down, ain't no discharge on the ground, sound off one two, sound off three four, break it on down, one two three four one two, three four." Another went like this, "Ain't no use in going home, Jody's got your gal and gone." Jody was a mythical character who did not participate in the war and took your girl back home away from you while you were away in the Army. Truth be told, it was not uncommon for guys to get "Dear John" letters from home as their girlfriends and sometimes even their wives told them their relationship was over since they could not wait for their partner to return home.

It was not uncommon for guys to collapse during training due to heat stroke and one in our squad died because of it. One day a new company moved in next door to us that was apparently a Mississippi National Guard unit in training. National Guard units were held in low esteem by us and were mainly a means for many men to "play Army on the weekends" and avoid real service in the war. National Guard service did not always guarantee one would not serve in Vietnam. One of my friends in Vietnam was married and joined the Guard to be able to remain at home with his family. However, soon after joining the guard, his unit in the states was activated into full time duty and was assigned to Germany. He had one year remaining on his six-year obligation only to be transferred to Vietnam for that last year. Fortunately, his marriage remained strong and his wife wrote him faithfully almost every day.

The Mississippi unit carried a big flag with the State Flower, the magnolia, on it. Instead of making the ten-mile march to the rifle range like us, they were trucked there and would pass us on the road each day laughing and making fun of us struggling along in the intense heat on the ground. We called them the "flower girls" as an insult. One morning our DI asked if we wanted to show up those "sissies" and we eagerly agreed. We purposefully waited for them to leave ahead of us in their trucks with their flag waving, then we broke ranks and ran, following our DI on a shortcut through the woods and back trails to the rifle range where we waited in formation for the "girls" to arrive, exhausted but with big grins as they tried to figure out how we beat them on foot!

After being assigned to a basic training battalion, I was given the top bed of one of the twenty or so bunk beds in a barracks where we were known as the "Third Herd", meaning we were squad number three of the four basic training squads making up Company A of a training battalion. The morning of day number one our drill sergeant woke us up at about 4:00 AM with orders to get up and dressed in less than 3 minutes or suffer the consequences. In an attempt to follow instructions, I jumped out of the top bunk, fractured both ankles and suffered constant pain for the remainder of the training cycle. I somehow endured the pain through sheer will power in order to avoid having to start the entire process again after being placed on "light duty" for an extended period. That was a real "character" builder for me that would serve me well the rest of my life. I left basic in the best physical condition of my life and weighed a sleek 135 pounds, a weight I would not see again!

Once when we were out in the field for several days on bivouac and unable to bathe for days, our DI told us we were going to march in formation 2 to 3 miles where we would be allowed to shower. He also told us to strip naked, wearing only our boots, drape a towel over our right shoulder and hold a bar of soap in our left. We proceeded to march in formation to the showers, completely naked, keeping perfect time and singing various cadence songs. What a sight that must have been! You soon learned there was no place for modesty in the Army.

I was one of the few who brought a modest amount of money with me and soon discovered a profitable side venture, lending cash. It began with someone asking to borrow $10.00 until payday. I agreed, but stipulated he pay $15.00 back, $10.00 was a return of principal and the $5.00 extra was a "service charge". After a few days I had others asking for loans until payday and I instantly recognized the opportunity, but I also knew I would need a "collector". I had befriended a big black kid from Mississippi we all knew as "Big John" when I shared my water with him on a long, hot march back to the barracks after a day of training and he had run out of water in his canteen. He gladly took the job for a modest commission since we had become friends. The beginnings of a career in banking had begun without my even realizing it. Some might call it "loan sharking", but I prefer calling it the "payday" loan business.

Before basic was finished, it was time to get our immunization and vaccination shots for protection against a wide variety of illnesses that were common in less developed countries around the world. I expected maybe a couple of shots from a syringe, but what followed was totally unexpected. We were told to remove our shirts, tie them around our waist and to single file through the designated building and keep our hands firmly against our sides. When we reached the front of the line, four people, two on each side, placed a strange looking device against our shoulders. The devices resembled what we know now as a nail gun which had a compressed air hose attached to it and a glass bottle situated on top that was filled with vaccination serum. At the count of three, four triggers were pulled simultaneously, forcing the serum into our arms at the same time. The force of the air-injected serum caused most of us to walk out of the building bleeding from both shoulders with severe pain. Some guys even fainted before they left the building, but we had been vaccinated for most diseases we would come into contact around the world.

Basic training was over in 6 weeks. One of our DIs told us he had been very tough because he had been to Vietnam and knew what awaited us and he wanted to make us as prepared as possible before we were thrown into the melee.

Finally, everybody received orders for their next duty station and most were instructed to report to Advanced Individual Training at various posts in different specialties, but the most common one was for Infantry training at Ft. Polk. To my surprise I was ordered to report to Key West, Florida for "On the Job Training", OJT. On the job training for what I had no idea.

KEY WEST

During basic training, I had become friends with a boy from Birmingham, Alabama named Ozzie, and we both received orders to report to Key West, Florida for OJT. Needless to say, we were jubilant about the prospect of doing duty of any kind in Key West since we both had expected to go straight into advanced infantry training at Ft. Polk like most of our comrades. Ozzie was newly married with a small baby at home and after graduation from basic training, he and his wife offered me a ride as far as Birmingham, Alabama which was their home. In Birmingham, I bought a ticket on Greyhound to take me to Tifton and was picked up by my parents for a few days at home before the trip to Key West.

Before entering service, I had purchased a new Pontiac from Childs Cadillac-Pontiac dealership in Tifton for $2,300.00 with payments of $100.00/ month. I was very proud of that car because it was my first new car and it was considered very sporty at the time, and because I was paying for it myself. It was a two door with the latest gadgetry, factory air conditioning, AM/FM radio and a built in 8 track tape player! On the appointed day sometime in late July or early August 1968, I loaded up my car for the trip to sunny Key West, stopping first in Tallahassee, Florida to pick up my friend Ozzie who had flown there from Birmingham. We proceeded South down the Florida West Coast having a ball with that 8 track player blaring the latest hit tunes by Janice Joplin, Jimmie Hendrix, The Doors and many others. We assumed when we reached Miami it would be a short drive down the Keys, but we were very wrong! It was a long, slow 160 mile drive south from Miami on a narrow two lane road with heavy traffic in both directions. It was truly an overseas highway with the only bridges spanning wide stretches being the remains of the old Florida East Coast Railway bed built by Henry Flagler. It was truly a "white knuckle" drive across those railroad bridges with the only barrier from the ocean below being the crude guard rails made from the remains of the old railroad that had been mounted to the side of the bridge. The railway originally terminated in Miami, but Mr. Flagler extended it as far as Key West and had planned to extend it to Havana, Cuba across 90 miles of open ocean.

Our orders stated we were to report to an Army Hawk Missile Battery at the Key West Naval Air Station located on a small island adjacent to Key West called Boca Chica. Key West was a dream come true with beautiful scenery, modern new barracks and a casual relaxed atmosphere. This duty station was very unusual because it had Army, Navy, Marine, Airforce and Coast Guard personnel stationed on the same base, with smaller units posted all over the islands of the southern Keys. The Army had established a missile defense detachment there in the early 1960s following the Cuban Missile Crisis that occurred under President John Kennedy.

Ozzie and I were both assigned to the Headquarters detachment and performed routine clerical duties since we were both able to use a typewriter. In those days, the latest typing equipment was an IBM Selectric that was electrically powered with the letters stamped onto a round ball that revolved with each stroke. However, most of the typing duties required multiple carbon paper copies since copying machines had not yet been invented. Copies had to be made using carbon paper and any mistype on the original could usually be corrected with an erasure, but the copies could not be corrected satisfactorily, thereby resulting in the need to retype the entire document since the Army required each document be perfect or near perfect. I worked in the office of the commanding officer, a Lieutenant Colonel. Duty there was very easy and we had a lot of fun during that summer and fall. At night, we could simply go outside our barracks to an estuary of the Atlantic and catch fresh shrimp and routinely have shrimp boils! Some of the guys would occasionally borrow scuba equipment from the recreation department and catch fresh lobster around the bridge pilings of the overseas highway. We ate in the Navy mess hall and the food there was the best I had in the military. Occasionally people from the different services would get confused about each other's rank since the ranking stripes were completely different. Sometimes I would get saluted by Navy personnel who could not figure out my rank. I was still the lowest ranking

Private in the Army with absolutely no ranking stripes and I would always proudly salute back, confusing them even more.

On payday, the first of each month we would file into the Navy Finance Office and pick up our month's pay in the form of a government check, then I would drive a group into downtown, for a modest fee of course, to a bank in Key West to cash them. Every pay day a man named Mel Fisher, a former poultry farmer from Arkansas, would be outside the bank with a small booth trying a sell stock in a company he started to explore for Spanish treasure off the coast of the Florida Keys. I listened to his sales pitch several times, but was never convinced to part with any of my precious $92.00 monthly pay. I remember him saying he was on the trail of a legendary shipwreck called the Atocha, which had sailed from South America on its way to Spain, but was caught in a hurricane and sank on the coral reefs between Key West and Havana, Cuba. Ship's manifests in Spain documented the ship was loaded with tons of precious jewels along with tons of gold and silver and other articles of almost immeasurable value. This missed opportunity turned out later to be one of the biggest investment mistakes I ever made. Mr. Fisher, several years later, found the elusive Atocha and recovered literally tons of priceless Spanish gold and silver coins and jewelry worth untold millions. Everyone who invested in his company shared in the treasure by receiving a portion of the loot he recovered for their share. There is still a Mel Fisher museum in Key West filled with many of the beautiful artifacts he recovered.

In November that year, one of our buddies decided he would catch a plane from the small Key West airport and fly home, without permission, to spend Thanksgiving with his family since we were off duty until the following Monday. He had very bad luck that day because his plane was highjacked by a Cuban refugee on the flight to Miami and he was taken to Havana, Cuba. He was later released and returned to Key West with live TV from Key West showing the passengers deplaning and our buddy was front and center of the coverage! He was appropriately punished but was known thereafter as "bad luck Charlie". Everybody was eventually given a nickname and at times I was known as the Georgia Peach, other times as the Professor. Ozzie's wife had moved to Key West to join him with their baby and lived in a very small, cheap apartment in Key West. She cooked a Thanksgiving dinner that year and invited me and a couple of other buddies over to share in the meal. We all appreciated that gesture and sense of "family" very much. We knew they had very little money and we all insisted they take payment to help with the cost of food.

Sometime around Christmas of 1968 Ozzie and I both received orders that we were being reassigned for duty in Vietnam. It was very strange how our short careers in the military had kept us connected. We were to have 30 days leave before shipping out for our overseas assignments. The inevitable had finally come and I made the long drive home with Ozzie and his family following me up I-75 as far as Lenox. They had dinner with me at my parent's home before continuing up I-75 through Atlanta and on to Birmingham. I knew Ozzie had been assigned to some unit in Vietnam, but we lost track of each other and never made contact again.

Military Pay Chart 1969

During the second session of the 91st. Congress, Public Law 91-231 was passed which provided for a 12.6% pay raise for the uniformed members of the Armed Forces.

| 1968 Pay | | 1970 Pay | | Pay Raises |

The United States military pay scales below became effective on July 1, 1969 and continued to be in effect until December 31, 1969. It is the basic pay amounts for the active components of the Navy, Marines, Army, Air Force, Coast Guard.

The pay rates are monthly, US dollar.

Enlisted pay for less than 2 to over 6 years of service.

Pay Grade	Years of Service				
	Under 2	Over 2	Over 3	Over 4	Over 6
E-7	342.30	410.10	425.40	440.40	455.40
E-6	294.90	358.20	372.90	388.20	403.20
E-5	254.70	313.80	328.80	343.20	365.70
E-4	214.20	268.50	283.50	305.70	321.00
E-3	155.10	216.30	231.30	246.30	246.30
E-2	127.80	179.10	179.10	179.10	179.10
E-1	123.30	163.80	163.80	163.80	163.80

Enlisted pay chart for 8 to over 16 years of service.

Pay Grade	Years of Service				
	Over 8	Over 10	Over 12	Over 14	Over 16
E-9		648.90	663.90	679.20	694.20
E-8	544.50	559.80	574.50	589.80	604.80
E-7	469.80	484.80	500.40	522.60	537.30
E-6	417.90	433.20	455.40	469.80	484.80
E-5	380.70	395.70	410.10	417.90	417.90
E-4	321.00	321.00	321.00	321.00	321.00
E-3	246.30	246.30	246.30	246.30	246.30
E-2	179.10	179.10	179.10	179.10	179.10
E-1	163.80	163.80	163.80	163.80	163.80

The chart above shows the monthly pay scale for enlisted members of the military during 1969. In addition, the government "generously" added another $50.00 to $65.00 each month as a "combat" pay bonus. These are gross monthly figures before any withholding taxes such as social security, state and federal income taxes. Not much pay for these men for the sacrifices they would face in the war.

THE JOURNEY BEGINS

My tour of duty began in February 1969 with my family seeing me off at the Atlanta International Airport. I had a heavy duffle bag packed full of clothing, much of which would later be discarded since it was of no use where I was going. The huge airport was filled with GIs of every branch of service either going to war or returning home from it. It was easy to tell which category these men fit into just by looking at them and the expression on their faces. We seemed to be invisible to most of the people we encountered and I wondered what was so wrong about wearing our military uniforms. Even airport employees just wanted us out of the way, especially with so many of us taking up space on the airlines using military standby payment vouchers, meaning our flights were being paid for by the Department of Defense and they couldn't make as much money off our flights. I was apprehensive, of course, about what lay ahead, but I absolutely believed it would have no effect on me and would only be a small blip on my way to the top.

Once I boarded the plane, it was only a matter of a few hours until I landed at the San Francisco International Airport. I arrived in San Francisco a day in advance of my date to report to the Oakland Army Base, so I decided to hail a taxi at the airport and make my way over the bay to the City of Oakland and have one last big meal and a night in a good clean bed. I asked the taxi driver to take me to Oakland to a good hotel. As soon as he dropped me off at one of Oakland's finest hotels, I instantly knew this was a big mistake. There were no "nice" hotels in Oakland. I had been dropped off at a flop house. I stupidly paid cash for one night and went up to my room which had holes in the walls, roaches climbing the walls and loud arguments all around only partially deafened by the paper-thin walls. I really didn't feel safe so I went back to the front lobby and was told by the desk clerk there would be on refunds and taxi service was not available in this area, but he did point me in the right direction to a taxi stand at least 10 city blocks away. I finally made it out of the area on foot, carrying the heavy duffle bag, without getting mugged and was able to flag down a taxi.

Whenever I recall this time, I remember two popular songs of the day, "Sitting on the top of the bay" by Otis Redding of Georgia and "If you're going to San Francisco" by Scott McKensie and Cass Elliott with their group known as the "mamas & the papas". After flagging down a taxi, I made my way over the old Bay Bridge, found a nice hotel and enjoyed a good meal and a restful, safe night's sleep before reporting to the Oakland Replacement Center the next day. The next several days consisted of a lot of "hurry up and wait", processing. Replacement centers like this were always unpleasant places to be. There seemed to be an endless stream of young GIs, creeping through endless lines, being issued new jungle fatigues, boots and etc. with most of us being issued jungle clothing that did not fit, but the objective was to rush as many "lambs" to the slaughter as fast as possible. I remember being assigned duty late one night to pass out two pair of jungle boots to each GI snaking his way through the line. I was precariously perched on top of a huge pile of boots and as someone below would ask the customer what size he wore, that information was shouted up to me. With no organization to the pile, it was necessary to plunder around looking for the proper size, so after a few minutes of this, I would just pickup up a pair of whatever size was handy and tossed them down. If they didn't fit, the customer was told to swap with someone else, but to keep moving because the line had to continue. Unlike earlier in the war when whole divisions were sent into battle as a group, we were replacements and very diversified in military backgrounds, some of us were new to military service and some had many years of experience, coming from duty stations all over the world to be assigned to new units in Vietnam.

After completing this portion of the journey, approximately 300 of us boarded a TWA plane at San Francisco International Airport on February 22, 1969 that had been specifically outfitted to pack as many GIs inside as possible, since the airline was being paid a hefty $3,000.00 per head for a one way trip. Everybody was apprehensive about the journey before us, but we remained upbeat, laughing and joking, much like whistling through a dark cemetery alone at night. One bright spot were the pretty young stewardesses who accompanied us to Honolulu.

We arrived at Honolulu International Airport sometime during the night to refuel and restock. We were allowed to wait in the nice, new terminal building, feeling very much at home in familiar surroundings and hearing our native language. Little did we know how much things were going to change for the worse in just a few hours.

The flight out of Honolulu brought in a new stewardess crew, not so young and not so pretty. The next stop was also during the night at the tiny island of Guam, a small dot in the middle of the vast western Pacific. The "airport terminal" turned out to be a crude ramshackle structure with absolutely no resemblance to the modern facilities we had just left. I picked up a copy of the latest military newspaper, "The Stars and Stripes" and read that the flight just ahead of us had taken hostile fire on their approach into the airport in Vietnam, but there was no mention whether there had been casualties or not. I had occupied the window seat up to that point and my seatmate kept asking to swap places so he could get a better view out the window. After learning of the ground fire taken by the previous flight, I told him he could have the cherished window seat, thinking his body would offer at least some protection if small arms fire came from the side of the plane as we were landing. I know that was stupid and self-serving, but he was overjoyed!

Again, the stewardess crew changed and now consisted of what looked like retired military drill sergeants with absolutely no personality or humor. The final leg of the flight began and most of the laughter and joking had stopped as everyone realized we were about to enter an entirely different world from any we had ever known, a country most of us had not heard of only a few years earlier. Dawn began to break as we approached land, and I saw two Air Force fighter jets take up station nearby with one off each wingtip to provide escort to our final destination of the flight, Bien Hoa Airbase. Daybreak arrived and I saw waves breaking on the beaches of Vietnam below. Beyond the shoreline, I could see small fires burning for miles into the distance and bomb craters making it look like a strange pockmarked place, sort of like something out of Dante's "Inferno". My first thoughts were "what an evil and foreboding place this must be", and my worst fears were soon born out. A short while later, the pilot told us we were going to land in a few minutes and for everyone to be seated, strapped in, and prepare for a very steep descent into the airport since he wanted to stay high in the air for as long as possible to minimize the chance of being hit by ground fire from below. I had no idea a commercial airliner could dive at such a steep angle, but this pilot had obviously done this before, and he had a healthy fear of being shot. We were soon on the ground with tanks lining the runway on both sides for added protection for the big, vulnerable airliner. I made a mental note the date was February 23rd, 1969 and I began to mark off each day thereafter.

Shortly after landing, the exit ramp was lowered and we began to file out and down the steps to face whatever awaited. I immediately saw a small, tin building near us with a sign over the door that read, "Graves Registration". A young GI behind me whispered to himself, "What in hell have I got into now?" I think all of us had the same thought. In front of the building was a flat topped trailer with six aluminum caskets, sitting alone, baking in the already hot sun with no flags, no honor guard or escort, waiting to be loaded into the cargo hold of our plane as if they were just another load to be hauled back home. The sight sent a cold chill down my spine as the reality of war was becoming all too real and apparent. A sergeant waited for us to unload and gather together for instructions. He greeted us with a derisive "Welcome to Vietnam, ladies," and among other things, he reminded us there were only two ways back home. One was to do our time, do whatever we were told and walk back up the steps of another plane, or be loaded into the cargo hold of a plane for an early return in a casket. His words and the scorching heat were like a sobering slap in the face! We were then directed to a crude, tin "terminal building" to await the arrival of the cattle trucks, "deuce and a halves", or cargo trucks that were to arrive, pick us up and haul us to the next stop of the trip, the army replacement center at Long Binh Army Base, some 5 to 10 miles away. Long Binh was the largest U.S. military installation in the world at that time and included restaurants, bowling alleys, movie theatres, swimming pools and a Country Club with a golf course open to officers of the rank of Brigadier General and above. The Army's in-country jail was known to the troops as the LBJ, a play on the words "Long Binh Jail, and Lyndon B. Johnson." Inside the terminal building, we saw the veterans who had finished their tours and were waiting for us to unload so they could board their "Freedom Bird" for the flight back home, "back to the world" as it was called. The two groups looked vastly different. We walked by them with fresh haircuts, clean shaven, new uniforms and shiny new boots, looking rested and well fed.

They, on the other hand, looked thin, exhausted, unshaven and wearing dirty, faded fatigues that had been worn thin. We didn't speak to them, nor they to us. It was obvious these young men had seen and done things no young man should ever have to see or do. We didn't know what to say to them because the looks in their eyes seemed to say it all. We knew that after our tour, we would probably look like them when our tours ended, if we were lucky enough to survive. Unlike veterans of World War II, we would all return home to be greeted with dishonor, rebuke and disrespect. Most would bring the ghosts of Vietnam back with them and would never fully be able in their mind to leave Vietnam behind. More than 58,000 young Americans would make the trip back home alone, in a bright aluminum casket. The average age of the Vietnam serviceman was only 19, too young to legally buy a beer, but not too old to die in a faraway land, fighting to rescue a people who for the most part resented us, did not want us there and just wanted to be left in peace, while we represented a nation back home that simply did not care. After about an hour, we were told the trucks had been delayed because the Viet Cong controlled the highway from Bien Hoa to Long Binh and the road would have to be cleared before we could depart. I was assigned duty in a few days with the 1st Infantry Division, and made the trip there in in another cattle truck. Our destination was base camp DiAn. All along the road, kids would come out and greet us with the "finger" and some would shout out they would sell their little sister for sex for a couple of dollars.

That year changed my life forever, as it did most who served there, experiencing sheer terror at times and laughing and joking with newly made friends, who likely would not see each other again, but the comradeship we shared was without equal. These newly made friends would not hesitate to sacrifice their very lives, if necessary, for their comrades because they knew their comrades would do the same for them. It was up to us to make it out alive, there was no one else. I learned lessons that year which have remained with me to this day, including a personal experience with God I cannot quite describe. Vietnam was an unpopular war at the time, as well as the brave young men who fought there, but I take great pride having stepped forward and served my country when it was popular not to.

So it was on day one, only 364 more to go.

BASE CAMP DI AN, VIETNAM

T he 1st Infantry Division is the oldest active duty division still serving the country, stationed in Fort Riley, Kansas. It was founded in 1917 under General John J. Pershing and fought gallantly in World War I in Europe. In World War II the division was first to land on many of the invasion sites, including Omaha Beach on D Day and subsequently earned the nickname, "The Bloody First" because of all the fierce battles they engaged in. The division shoulder patch thereafter became a big, red, numeral 1 and I was proud to serve with this famous outfit. The division motto is "No Mission too Difficult, No Sacrifice Too Great, Duty First".

I was finally assigned my weapon, the Colt M-16 assault rifle. This was a revolutionary new rifle design and was loved by some, hated by others. Whether you loved it or hated it depended on what model you were issued. The .30 caliber M-1 Carbine became widely used in the Korean War. However, the drawback of the M-1 in combat was that it was seriously under-powered. As a result of this, American weapons designers concluded that a small-caliber, high velocity round would be more effective in combat. Experts were bitterly divided on what a new assault rifle should be like. It was finally decided that the new weapon, the M-14 would be the same caliber, 7.62 mm, as the concurrent new standard machine gun. The M-14 was said by testers at the Army's Springfield Armory to be the best ever tested at its facility. Subsequently, the M-14 rifle and the M-60 machine gun were both approved as standard Army issue weapons.

The first tests of the M-14 in combat in Vietnam versus the AK-47 used by the enemy proved the M-14 was uncontrollable in automatic firing mode and soldiers could not carry enough ammunition to maintain firepower superiority over the enemy. While the M-2 carbine offered a high rate of fire, it was under-powered. It became apparent that a replacement was needed. The Army was forced to find a replacement weapon and a request in 1957 by General Willard Wyman to develop a .223 inch caliber, select fire rifle weighing 6 pounds when loaded with a full 20 round magazine was reconsidered. The new weapon had to penetrate a standard U.S. helmet at 500 yards and retain a velocity in excess of the speed of sound, while matching or exceeding the wounding ability of the .30 Carbine cartridge.

That request ultimately resulted in the Armalite AR-15 rifle. The Armalite AR-15 used .22 caliber bullets which destabilized when they hit a human body, unlike the .30 caliber round, which typically passed through in a straight line. The smaller caliber meant it could be controlled in autofire mode due to the reduced recoil. The AR-15 could fire 600 to 700 rounds a minute with an extremely low jamming rate. Parts were stamped out, not hand machined, so it could be mass-produced, and the stock was plastic to reduce weight.

In 1963, Secretary of Defense Robert McNamara concluded that the AR-15 was a superior weapon to others tested and ordered a halt to M-14 production. Mass production of the weapon soon began. Modifications soon followed that resulted in the M-16 version that was air cooled, gas operated, magazine fed assault rifle made of steel and aluminum alloy and composite plastics, truly cutting edge at the time. The new weapon was touted to the troops as being a self-cleaning rifle that needed no basic upkeep. Subsequently, the Army did not even supply soldiers cleaning equipment for the rifle. In the heat, humidity and dirt of the jungles of Vietnam soon proved that claim to be false.

In McNamara's haste to introduce the new weapon into use, short-cuts were taken to produce the rifle in mass numbers and it was prone to jam easily in combat situations. One notable deficiency was the lack of a chrome plated chamber which reduced the rust and corrosion that caused the rifle to jam frequently. One Marine reported his 72 man platoon left on a mission and returned with only 19. He said what killed most of them was their own rifle. Almost all the dead men were found with their M-16 torn down trying to fix them.

Another early deficiency of the weapon was the gun powder used in the cartridge. The gun powder used caused corrosion and residue build up in the chamber, resulting in jamming problems.

All these problems were eventually corrected and a superior weapon, the M-16 A1 was lightweight, fired a 5.56 mm NATO round and was adopted no only by the U.S. military, but also by many nations worldwide.

I trained with the M-14 in basic, but the M-16 soon became my favorite. My second favorite weapon was the M-79 grenade launcher that fired a 40MM sized grenade, good for maybe up to a range of 100 yards. It made a characteristic "thumping" sound when fired and was known to us as "The Thumper", making an impressive blast when it exploded. The one weapon I feared most was the hand grenade, due to the extreme danger it posed in accidentally detonating on the user. I admit, on occasions, to throwing grenades into streams of water just to see the underwater explosion and what strange looking fish or other animals might float to the surface. You learned to get entertainment whenever and wherever you were at the time.

Base camp Di An was one of many established by the 1st Infantry when they first deployed to Vietnam in October, 1965. Army engineers cleared the site from dense jungle after first killing off all the vegetation with agent orange. Then they would bulldoze the entire area to provide a clear field of fire for defensive protection and begin construction of buildings, hooches, mess halls and etc. It was located near the small Vietnamese village of Di An. Also stationed nearby was a detachment of South Korean troops who served in Vietnam as a valuable ally. The South Vietnamese especially feared the South Korean troops and would vanish whenever the Korean troops left their compound on patrol. They knew the Koreans were very aggressive and would fire first and ask questions later.

Several 1st Division battalions operated out of Di An including infantry "grunts", the backbone of the Army. There were also air mobile troops that flew on search and destroy missions further out in the new "jeep" of the day, the Huey Helicopter. Others included heavy armor with tanks and APCs, armored personnel carriers along with combat engineers and artillery battalions. 1st Infantry, along with most other combat divisions of the day consisted of approximately 20,000 troops and was assigned a large geographic area of operations north of Saigon stretching from the Cambodian border east toward the coast of the South China Sea. Our mission was to act as a blocking force to deter the infiltration of North Vietnamese troops, equipment and supplies coming south along the Ho Chi Minh trail through Cambodia with Saigon as their ultimate target. I was assigned to the 1st Administration Company on the west side of the camp. Division headquarters was located about 50 miles further north at Base Camp Lai Khe, smack in the middle of an abandoned Michelin rubber tree plantation and was commanded by two star General A. E. Milloy. Colonel George Patton, Jr., son of the famous World War II General, commanded an armored battalion there also. The location of any base there made absolutely no sense because the South Vietnamese government had declared the rubber plantation to be a "no fire zone" because they wanted to preserve the rubber trees for future farming operations after the war. The designation as "no fire zone" meant it was a safe sanctuary for the VC and our forces could not pursue them or take offensive actions unless fired on first. The VC would infiltrate the area knowing they had reached sanctuary and fire rockets and mortars into Lai Khe, then disappear. It was known to those who served there as "Rocket City".

I arrived in DiAn during the dry season and wondered why there were so many deep gullies and washed out roads. The earth was similar to the red clay of Georgia and was extremely dry and dusty, causing me to sneeze uncontrollably at times. Any movement of vehicles, particularly helicopters, stirred up great clouds of red dust that covered everything nearby. The weather was witheringly hot and humid, but almost no rain. Later that fall I found out what the monsoon rains were all about. It would rain heavily once or twice every day, sometimes all day, then clear up with blazing sun and 110 – 120degree temperatures.

At times, the rainfall was a welcomed event, since it provided an opportunity to soap up and wash some of the grime from your body in the rain, including the white salt deposits left by excessive sweating that irritated the skin. It was important to take salt tablets regularly in response to the body excreting so much fluid in an attempt to keep itself cooled. You always hoped the rain would last long enough to wash the soap off before it stopped. At least we had a chance for a little sleep out of the rain whenever we could spend a night in the hooch. During the monsoons, however, rain would often come in during a blowing storm so you might as well be trying to sleep outside. I was very fortunate to have a cousin whos' wife helped manage a Holiday Inn. One day I received a large "care package" from them that contained bars of soap, plastic drinking glasses and some plastic shower curtains we used to seal off the areas of the ceiling where the rain was coming in. Of course, the shower curtains had the distinct Holiday Inn logo and name on them that brought us a lot of envy. If asked which hooch we slept in, we would brag we lived in the Holiday Inn!

It took my body at least a couple of months to adjust to the extreme temperatures. There was very little time off, with the average day filled with 12 to 16 hours at one task or another.

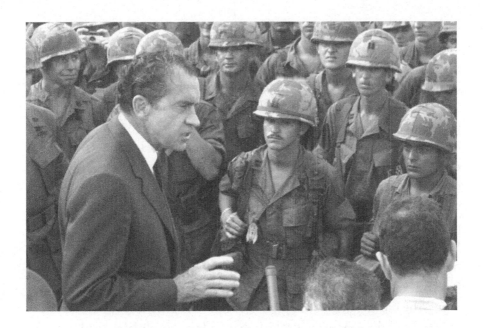

President Nixon with 1st Inf Div, Di An 1969

July 1969 brought an unexpected visit to 1st Infantry Division by the Commander-in-Chief, President Richard Nixon. We were told early in the day that we would have a special visitor and to prepare for inspection. Everything was to be spic and span with all equipment thoroughly cleaned, our jungle fatigues were to be the best we had, even our perimeter bunkers were to be ready for an intense inspection. We worked feverously all day in preparation for the visitor, but we were not told who it might be, just a "big wig". Later in the day, I was hunkered down in my bunker with the M-60 machine guns ready for action when I saw a flight of about eight helicopters approaching my position overhead. They caught my attention because it contained one particular chopper in the center surrounded by heavily armed gunships. The entourage continued overhead and landed about a mile from my position. We later learned the special visitor had been President Nixon.

President Nixon had been elected in November 1968 and inaugurated in January 1969. He ran on the promise that if elected, he would begin to unwind the American presence in Vietnam. The devastating reports each night on the news networks of the persistently high casualty reports suffered by our troops had taken their toll on the American public and resulted in a loss of political will to continue the war. The American people simply could not understand why so many young men had to die in this conflict which no one really understood.

The newly elected President began to make good on his campaign promise by changing the accepted strategy up to that point. The American casualty reports dropped significantly beginning in early 1969 as combat operations changed significantly. Enemy body count was no longer considered the measure of success. Nixon's goal was to find an end to the war and bring American troops back home. First, he took the war to the people of North Vietnam. Wave after wave of B-52 bombers flew over Hanoi and Haiphong harbor dropping their lethal loads on military targets below. The harbor was mined in order to stop the inflow of Russian and Chinese vessels bringing weapons and supplies to the North Vietnamese army. The North Vietnamese people began to experience for the first time, the might of the American military that had previously been held in check by President Lyndon Johnson. The fear of the Johnson administration was America had to be careful with our use of force since we might widen the war by provoking China and Russia. Both countries were supplying the North with weapons and even had troops stationed in the North manning anti-aircraft weapons systems and the like. Nixon authorized search and destroy missions into the former safe sanctuaries of Cambodia which had been off limits to American troops up until that point. Nixon's "Operation Linebacker" ultimately brought the North Vietnamese to the bargaining table in Paris and led to the withdrawal of American forces from Vietnam.

In the end, the government of South Vietnam collapsed and the North Vietnamese took control and united the whole peninsula. The long, fruitless war was finally over, leaving death and destruction in its wake. Its legacy remains to this day with the survivors and the families of the dead and wounded of both sides.

Many days were not average and lasted longer, seven days each week. At night, the mosquitoes would almost drive a person insane but the insect repellant the Army issued was very effective. Many times we didn't want to use it when we left camp because it had an odor the VC could recognize and pin point our presence. They could smell us primarily because of our diets, the smell of our soap or cigarettes, and we could smell them with their "sour fish" odor from their steady diet of fish and rice. Unlike us, with our very limited diets, the Vietnamese ate anything that walked, crawled, swam or flew, ANYTHING! They consumed rats, snakes, eels, and insects. The country also produced a lot of fruit and vegetables so there wasn't much excuse for being hungry if you didn't mind what you were eating. Some of the few times in my life I have actually known real hunger was in Vietnam and I began to understand the wisdom of their ability to survive in a hostile environment with little food, except what nature provided. When going through their villages, I would notice dogs at many family huts that were caged so they could fatten them up for one of their favorite treats, dog. After a few months, the mosquitoes seemed to abate a little, perhaps as my body adjusted to the environment. The army provided a big orange pill every morning to be taken to prevent a non-lethal type of malaria, only trouble was, it caused sudden, severe stomach cramps and diarrhea that would set in within a couple of hours after ingesting and it was not effective against a strain that was life threatening. There was no prevention for the type that would kill you, so most of us decided it was better to chance getting malaria than go through the same routine every day. With malaria, you would at least be able to spend some time out of the country, usually at an army hospital in Phillippines. The veterans would watch the incoming replacement troops taking the orange pills and place bets on how long it would take for the first "victims" to run for the outhouse, some making it in time and some not.

OUTHOUSE DISPOSAL SYSTEM

Life in camp with little or no rank was often not very pleasant. Wherever people are housed there has to be basic sanitation in order to prevent disease. Basic toilet facilities consisted of outhouses with six toilet seats and fifty-five gallon barrels underneath each hole that had been cut in half with handles attached on each side. The Vietnamese women, Mama Sans, would pull the containers out from the bottom to burn the contents. When the barrels were full, they had to be removed and the contents disposed of in a sanitary manner. In this case, diesel fuel was added to the "brew", stirred with a long handle, set on fire and burned to make the can ready for reuse. Obviously, this procedure must have been the genesis of the phrase, "To grab the s**t end of the stick", meaning a very grave mistake. The stench from this operation was absolutely nauseating, an odor stamped indelibly in the mind of any who experienced it. The Pacific Gas & Electric Company was a civilian contractor charged with providing this service. PG&E would hire local Vietnamese to do this most unpleasant task, but often they would just not show up for work, which I can easily understand, but it still had to be done. With nobody else left to do it, GIs were given this task, one I had to do on at least two occasions.

KP duty was another necessary task I was "blessed" to have in Vietnam. Local "Mama Sans" were hired to do many of the more dirty jobs like cleaning the huge pots used in the mess hall. On several occasions I carried a load out back for them to clean and watched as they cleaned the leftover food from inside, placed their dirty clothes in and proceed to do their laundry. When finished, they would swish a small amount of water inside and return the pot for the next meal. It usually required the passage of several days afterward until my appetite returned.

Another such necessary task was garbage collection and disposal. Makeshift garbage trucks would make their rounds periodically to pick up trash from inside camp and haul it to a nearby landfill. Vietnamese were hired to do this job, but they needed protection whenever they left the camp headed for the trash dump and back. Another reason for a guard on the truck was that we couldn't trust the ones going all through the camp. I was assigned the position as the "shotgun" rider a few occasions, but if the other workers needed to actually pick up trash from the ground and toss it atop the truck didn't show for work, we would have to fill in for them. In the heat of Vietnam, it didn't take long for trash to spoil with all manner of insects and rodents being attracted to it. The clouds of insects and the size of the rats were astonishing. One day I was assigned to the top of the truck to catch the trash containers being tossed up, empty them and waded around in the trash all day praying there would be at least a little water left to wash off. When we drove outside the camp to the garbage dump, there would be scores of Vietnamese searching through the trash looking for anything they might be able to save and possibly use for another purpose. They were ingenious at taking our trash and repurposing it for another use, sometimes even into weapons to be used against us.

Army regulations forbid mailing war "trophies" back home, but some items were especially prized, such as VC, Chinese or Russian flags. A friend showed me a new, AK-47 rifle he had captured in a nearby village during a patrol. It was still wrapped in the factory shipping paper. He was determined to get it back home even though it was strictly forbidden. The problem would be how to do it. He eventually came up with an ingenious plan. He disassembled the rifle and shipped the individual pieces one by one to his parents in separate packages which were never inspected. What a prize that has turned out to be!

At 1st Admin I was assigned duty in a section titled "Special Correspondence" and was sometimes known as Congressional Inquiries Section. My job was to receive the letters and telegrams from Congressmen and Senators inquiring about specific members of our Division who had complained about some real or imagined mistreatment. Typically, a soldier in Vietnam would write a family member back home that he had been assigned to some job he was not trained for or that he had some type of injury the army would not treat. The family member would naturally be enraged and forward the complaint to their Congressman who would then forward it to the Pentagon, then it was sent to MACV headquarters, Military Assistance Command Vietnam, and finally it wound up on my desk. My job was to find the soldier, interview him, wherever he might be, and investigate his complaint, remedy the situation if possible, and write a report of the findings and any action taken. My report was then reviewed by my superior, approved or sent back for further action on my part, then telegraphed back to the Congressman's office in Washington, D.C. This job required traveling to many of the far-flung camps and bases of the division under, at times, some very frightening circumstances. It also meant getting to the soldier by helicopter many times or by grinding through the field, if necessary. There was no internet or other instant form of written communication then except for Western Union Telegraph, and that was the communication link used while corresponding with the office that had initiated the inquiry. It seems very primitive by today's standard of instant news and communication.

I soon became very good at my job and was promoted to the position of head enlisted man in charge of about four other GIs in this section with the rank of Specialist 5, a non-commissioned officer. One perk of this rank was being able to eat in the Non-Com mess hall where the food was supposed to be a little better. My pay shot up to about $450.00/month which included overseas pay and combat zone pay! It was so extravagant, I would only keep $100.00 for monthly necessities, mostly beer, cigarettes and etc. I sent the rest home every month to be put into a savings account. We were not paid in U. S. dollars, but in Military Script that was of no value any place other than on a military installation in Vietnam. The Vietnamese accepted it as payment even knowing it's limited use. In order to prevent the counterfeiting of our script, the army would seal off entire

WARREN ROBINSON

bases on unannounced dates to exchange the old-style script for new. From that day onward, the old script was absolutely worthless. Whenever these events happened, the Vietnamese would gather outside the gates pleading with GIs to take their old script and swap it for the new issue at full face value with the GI taking a huge fee.

One of my assignments occurred during the monsoon season that required a visit to a remote artillery unit in the field near the Cambodian border. That night the camp was attacked and a fierce fire fight ensued that lasted at least an hour. After getting the information I needed the following day, I caught a helicopter flight out and we were soon caught in a driving monsoon rainstorm with visibility almost nonexistent. In those conditions, navigation became very difficult with no visual references to go by, the pilots relied on radio signals from beacons placed throughout the country. The pilots would fly from one beacon to the next, only problem was everybody else in the air was doing the same, making it very possible to crash into another chopper midair. Our pilot ordered us to strap up, lean out on both sides and look in every direction for any other traffic coming our way to help him avoid a midair collision. That method was not very realistic, but at least it gave us something to do. I soon learned from other more experienced GIs to sit on my flat jacket whenever traveling by air or land in hopes it would provide protection from small arms fire or shrapnel penetrating the bottom of the helicopter or vehicle floor and striking me in a very personal area of the body.

On another occasion, a young platoon leader was in command of performing a "Hammer & Anvil" maneuver. This maneuver was typically done at night. Part of the platoon would set up an ambush position along a trail leading out of a known or suspected Viet Cong village. The rest of the platoon would then begin a sweep through the village making noise, with the hope of driving the enemy inside the village into the ambush on the other side. The plan was executed, but there were no VC in the village, and the GIs sweeping through it triggered the ambush onto themselves by mistake as they entered the "kill zone" on the other side. The Lieutenant, son of a retired General, was wounded in the groin by shrapnel from an exploding claymore mine. It was not possible to stop the bleeding with a tourniquet due to the location of the wound, and he subsequently bled out and died before reaching the surgical hospital. I was sad to have the assignment of explaining this to his father. It was one time I was instructed to relay the entire story with none of the usual trite explanations.

Many families would receive notification their loved one had been killed in action with only a brief explanation of the circumstances and they wanted a more detailed account of what had taken place. My first instinct was to investigate and tell them the gruesome truth, oftentimes not what the Army wanted told, so I was instructed to write the reports saying the GI had died by enemy fire under heroic circumstances, which was not always true, but I later realized the wisdom of this practice since it let every surviving widow or parent hang on to a heroic memory of their loved one when the truth would have been a more bitter pill to swallow.

Another inquiry was concerning the whereabouts of a GI who had simply vanished, seemingly into thin air and his family had not heard from him for many months. I visited his outfit and made a lot of inquiries and several of his buddies told me he had become involved with a Vietnamese girl in Saigon, but they had no idea where he might be. The case puzzled me, but I was not able to get any further leads. There was no indication anything adverse had happened to him, but the case seemed to just stall. Then one night, the notion came to me to check his records and find out if he was still being paid. Payroll records showed someone was using his ID every month and receiving his pay. Next pay day, I had everybody alerted to find out who was drawing his pay. MPs waited at the payments desk when a GI showed up to draw the missing soldier's pay. My hunch was right and he had simply gone AWOL into Saigon and was living with his girlfriend! I don't know what happened to him after that, but he probably spent some time in the Long Binh Jail, maybe even prison in Fort Leavenworth, Kansas.

The first couple of months were definitely a time of adjustment, not only to the extreme heat, but to life in general. Everybody, at one time or another, contracted some type of skin malady due to the heat, humidity and filthy clothing, including the "jungle rot", where large patches of skin on the body would become infected with a fungus that would remove the skin pigmentation in the affected area leaving large white splotches all over the body. Other skin maladies would attack private areas of the body and would drive the victim almost insane. I have always had a healthy fear of snakes of any kind, so Vietnam was not good for me! Snakes seemed to be everywhere and none of them resembled the poisonous rattlesnakes of my native South Georgia, and we were told most of them were venomous and avoid them whenever possible. Avoiding snakes in Vietnam was an impossible task. They came in every size and color, but I did recognize the cobra and saw many during my tour. The cobra would often spew its venom at a victim, hitting the person in the eyes and temporarily blinding the victim.

The first time I knew I had been deliberately targeted by an enemy with the intent of killing me was during March or early April that year and suddenly the war became a very personal experience for me. It was very different from training when the fire was directed above your head.

Life at DiAn was not all bad and there were many good times there. There was a constant need for new sandbags to be used as protection from enemy fire and the company top sergeant routinely assigned the punishment of filling sandbags for even the slightest infraction. One day he surprised us by telling us at morning formation the whole company was being "invited" to a beer party he was throwing that day. We all knew what "being invited" meant so we showed up as ordered, expecting nothing but the worst. Sure enough, trucks had unloaded at least half a dozen loads of fresh dirt and there were stacks of empty sandbags and entrenching tools to fill them. I thought it was ironic that the sandbags had labels on them reading "Manufactured by Dowling Bag Co., Valdosta, Georgia", only 35 miles from my home. Top told us the party would begin as soon as we filled all those bags and we reluctantly started the task. The sun was baking hot and we sweated profusely only to have a little hot, terrible tasting water to drink. Then we saw a jeep pulling up with a large trailer attached, filled with ice and cold beer for the whole company!

On another occasion, Top told us we could have an enlisted men's club, but we had to build it ourselves. The finished "club" was made up of sandbags stacked up to a height of about 5 ft. in a large circle with a dirt floor and one entrance with no door and a large cargo parachute for a cover, held up in the center by a tall pole and ropes secured it to the ground on the outside. A makeshift bar was constructed from empty ammunition crates in one corner and a crude stage on the opposite side from the entrance. Crates were again stacked in rows and used as seating. An electric generator was "procured" from somewhere and was used to provide lighting and power for music. "Entertainment" was spotty at first since the USO wanted little to do with our "Club", but somebody engaged a Vietnamese group from somewhere in the area. The group did a pretty good imitation of current popular American rock tunes with an occasional comedian and a bad magic act, but in that environment, anything would have been great! The show always ended with the most popular event of the night, the Vietnamese striptease girls, who were always loudly cheered and received generous tips for their "performance". A crude sign was made and hung over the entrance proclaiming this place, "The Sandbagger", in honor of Top.

We listened as often as we could to Radio Station WAFVN (Armed Forces Viet Nam). It certainly was different from the ordinary civilian radio at the time. It aired news of the day along with such "motherly" advice as "change your socks often, or keep your weapon well cleaned, don't forget to take your malaria pills, salt tablets and etc". It even warned against the dangers of venereal disease. The station played the latest hit tunes and was very popular. Perhaps the most popular skit was one named "Checkenman". That was a radio series created by Dick Orkin that was a spoof of popular comic book heroes. Chickenman was created in 1966 on Chicago radio station WCFL. There were new episodes almost every day of about two minutes each. Each episode began with an overly dramatic theme, a four note trumpet sound followed by the chicken call "Buck-buck-buck-buuuuck" followed by a rousing cry of "Chickenmannn!" and voices shouting, He's everywhere! He's everywhere!"

We lived in "hooches", crude barracks facilities consisting of a concrete floor, walls that were framed up to a height of about 3 ft. and screened up to the ceiling from there. There was a tin roof with no ceiling underneath, only exposed rafters. One of the guys living with us had a pet monkey named "Doc", for some reason. Doc was very popular and was an accepted member of the hooch. One day we heard reports that VC Sappers were active in our area had killed several GIs in their sleep.

DOC

They were specially trained units that would enter through the defenses of camps at night, slip into hooches, slit the throats of GIs in their sleep, then vanish into the darkness. This naturally put everybody on edge at night. Doc liked to sleep in the rafters of our hooch and one night he went to sleep and fell onto a GI below who immediately assumed he was being attacked by a sapper. Utter pandemonium ensued with the "victim" screaming loudly and everybody scrambling around to grab their weapons and defend themselves. Doc became very unpopular after that and was banished from the hooch.

TYPICAL HOOCH

A new arrival to our hooch was a GI who had originally been assigned to the other side of the base with an armored unit as an APC driver. He had been ferrying field units out from Di An to various missions outside the camp and had been involved in 5 separate incidents where the APC he was driving encountered land mines, resulting in most of the occupants inside being badly wounded or killed, except him. He had been miraculously spared, with the exception of minor injuries each time. The last time he told his commanding officer he could not go out anymore and would take whatever disciplinary action given to him, including jail time, if necessary. Mercifully, he was assigned light duty after that and became a permanent daytime tower guard on the perimeter just behind our hooch. Having received 5 purple hearts, we dubbed him "Purply", and that became his moniker thereafter.

Sometime around mid-April that year, I was on guard duty, alone on a dark night after a lot of enemy activity in our area and scared to death. I couldn't help feeling sorry for myself and thinking I might never make it back home alive. I had been assigned a post that in effect, was human bait. Suddenly I heard a voice that I instantly knew to be God speaking to me saying, "Do not be afraid, I have other plans for your life and you will not die in this strange land". I first wondered if my mind had been playing tricks on me and I had just imagined what had happened, but I felt encouraged and later came to know it was definitely God that had given me his assurance. It would be many years later before I related this experience to anyone. Since that experience, I have had several confirmations of that promise.

MAJOR 1ST INFANTRY BATTLES

May 1967 thru December 1969

Various units of the Big Red One were engaged in 40 major battles during this time that resulted in the confirmed death count of 10,828 enemy soldiers along with thousands of weapons and supplies. Major battles included Toan Thang I and Toan II in March and April 1968 with more than 4,200 confirmed enemy kills along with Operation Atlas Wedge, An Loc I & An Loc II, Tight Squeeze and Thunder Road. With no clear strategy for seizing and holding territory, success was measured in Washington by the "body count" inflicted upon the enemy. The enemy, in contrast, had a very different measure of success saying that we could kill ten of their troops for every casualty we took, but they would win the war. They knew they could eventually win the political war with the American public.

One notable American casualty suffered during this period was the 1st Infantry Division Commanding Officer, Major General Keith L. Ware who was killed by hostile fire on September 13th, 1968 along with seven other soldiers accompanying him. General Ware's constant companion and faithful friend, King, died with his master. General Ware was a highly respected leader having been awarded the Medal of Honor for his heroism in World War II.

GENERAL WARE

WARREN ROBINSON

KING

THE MOON LANDING

J uly 20th, 1969 was a memorable day, with astronauts Neil Armstrong
and Buzz Aldrin becoming the first humans to set foot on the moon.
It began like any other day for me and in late afternoon I made myself
ready for my assignment that night, perimeter guard duty. Normally, I did
not look forward to this duty because it meant being up most, if not all,
of the night in all kinds of weather conditions and still having to report
for regular duty the next morning. But this day, I looked forward to it,
knowing the first moon landing ever was about to take place and there was
a clear night and a full moon to observe it. I took my position at a fortified
bunker on the perimeter wire along with two other GIs and we each took a
turn on watch as the other two slept, or at least rested. When my turn came
later that night, I could see the faint glow of the lights of Saigon to my
left. Directly in front of me about 10 miles away lay the Big Black Virgin
Mountain, where our troops occupied the top, but most of the remainder
was controlled by the VC. I could see our gunships circling the mountain,
spewing down what seemed to be an endless stream of red tracer fire on the
enemy below, in what must have seemed to them as if hell itself had been
unleashed against them. Off to my right maybe a mile away I could see
and hear a firefight taking place with red tracer fire, ours, going out and
green tracer fire, theirs, coming in. An 81mm mortar battery was almost
directly behind me about 200 yards and would sporadically let loose with
a deafening barrage of fire in support of our troops involved in the fight.
Directly behind me was a large open pit where human excrement from the
camp was dumped, mixed with diesel fuel and burned. The stench was
almost overwhelming. In the midst of all this chaos, I consciously made
the decision to burn these impressions in my mind. I wanted to remember
the noise and chaos of battle, the smell of blood, decaying bodies, the taste

of fear in my mouth. If I survived this journey, I knew someday I would fall into the trap of self-pity and I wanted to recall this moment and these memories to remind me that no matter what hurdles and setbacks life held in store for my future, I had survived worse times. I would cherish each new day God chose to give me on earth. Still I would gaze up at that bright moon and be in awe of this accomplishment by America. It made me proud to be an American and to be an American soldier. Looking back after 50 years, it is still considered a major technological achievement for mankind. It is unfortunate though that the same technology is being exploited today by several nations as a weapon of war.

REST & RECREATION

After 8 months in-country, I really needed a break and to be able to rest, unwind, relax and get into a friendlier environment. I, along with two buddies, decided to apply for permission to take our 7 day R&R. The available destinations included: Hong Kong, Kuala Lumpur, Honolulu Hawaii, Bangkok Thailand and Sydney Australia. Honolulu was almost exclusively reserved for married personnel and we were told there was a long waiting list for Sydney, Australia and we all felt we couldn't wait any longer having no assurance as to when we might be able to go. Through the process of elimination, the decision was made to sign up for Bangkok since it was available for immediate use. When our departure date came, we flew from Ton Son Nhut Air Base outside Saigon on an Air Vietnam flight with about $300.00 each that was burning a hole in our pockets. We were greeted in Bangkok with fresh face cloths that were soaked in ice water and fresh squeezed lemons and it felt like we had arrived in heaven! Three hundred U.S. dollars would buy a lot of luxury in Thailand and we took full advantage. We immediately hired a young man who offered his services for the week as a chauffeur, tour guide and general companion at the rate of about $30.00 each. He took us to a modern American style hotel where we booked separate rooms in anticipation of a few days of privacy, not having to bathe or take care of other bodily functions in front of dozens of other GIs. We also shed our uniforms and dressed in civilian clothing for the first time in a while. We took in several movies, our first since leaving home, went bowling, ate at nice restaurants with good American style food and toured most of the sights of Bangkok, including the floating market on the river, which this city is famous for. One day we drove south and spent a full day at a beautiful isolated beach on the Gulf of Thailand where we swam in the ocean and a local woman cooked us a delicious, fresh meal on the beach in a wok fueled by propane. Food never tasted so good!

Our 7 days were up far too soon, but we reluctantly made our way back to Vietnam, rested and in good spirits, dressed in our khaki uniforms as instructed. The first night back, we stayed in temporary barracks on the airbase waiting for a ride back to our unit, which was supposed to pick us up the next morning. Our convoy never showed up and we were told we would have to remain at Ton Son Nhut at least another day and maybe two. We became very restless and somebody came up with the hair-brained idea we could hitch hike our way back in convoys headed for bases in our general direction, it would be easy, they said. After making several inquiries with convoys leaving the base, one driver said he would drop us off close to our destination and we could easily catch another ride into Di An from there, since a lot of convoys would be headed that way. We hopped into the back of his truck with no weapons, no defenses and wearing our khaki uniforms, heading north through the huge city of Saigon and into the intimidating countryside beyond. The truck was well armed with a GI posted on top of the cab manning an M60 machine gun that had been attached to the cab of the truck for protection, with other trucks in front. In the middle of nowhere, our driver stopped at a fork in the road and told us we would have to dismount because he had to continue on to another base with his convoy, but not to worry, the next convoy would arrive in a few minutes, and pick us up for the final leg into Di An. More than an hour passed by and the next convoy never showed up, with darkness soon approaching. I have never felt more anxious in my life, totally defenseless in a very dangerous place where the enemy roamed freely after dark. A plan was formulated to find a hiding spot near the road, just inside the jungle and wait for morning. It wasn't very comforting, but it was the best we could come up with and we all knew we had to get off that road and do it fast. After finding our spot just before darkness fell, we heard a vehicle approaching our location. We decided to take our chances that it was a friendly and jumped onto the road, flagging down the driver who was indeed American and headed to our base camp! What a beautiful sight that truck was. I soon realized that truck did not just randomly come along and rescue us, it was sent from God who was saying to me, "Why were you so anxious, don't you remember my promise that your mission on earth was not yet finished?"

BOB HOPE AND CHRISTMAS 1969

A few days before Christmas, a special holiday treat was announced. Bob Hope and his USO show was going to make an appearance at First Division Headquarters in Lai Khe. Everyone would not be able to go, but I was one of the lucky ones selected. We made the trip in one large, long heavily armed convoy with Cobra Helicopter gunships flying overhead as escorts. There were more than 15,000 GIs waiting patiently for the show to begin when the guys sitting on the front row center were told they would have to move to the back to make room for some special guests to whom we all owed big thanks. They left with a lot of hissing and booing while a new group marched up to take their place. The Division Commander, General A. E. Milloy, took the stage and announced this group had been on routine patrol outside the base the night before and discovered 8 VC in the act of planting rockets to be used in an attack the following day when it would be filled with thousands of GIs. The crowd immediately erupted with enthusiastic applause and cheering! Accompanying Hope were, astronaut Neil Armstrong, singer-actress Connie Stevens, The Gold Diggers, Miss World 1969, Les Brown and his Band of Renown along with a juggling act. At the end of the show, we sang Christmas Carols and it was a truly great experience! I will always be grateful for Bob Hope and the USO for making this a most memorable Christmas away from home.

Some larger bases had regular USO shows but we didn't get to see many of those, so this Christmas show was fantastic. We considered Bob Hope and all the entertainers he brought with him as part of our "family". They donated their time at Christmas, to leave the safety of their lavish homes to be with us in very dangerous circumstances and gave us a reason to laugh. Another popular performer was Ann Margaret. She never turned down a request to entertain "her gentlemen", as she called them. We will always be grateful to Mr. Hope for making these shows possible.

Christmas Eve, I had guard duty again and was assigned two newcomers at my bunker. By that time, I had become a "short timer", meaning I had only a short time left to serve in-country. Every day I would cross the last one off my calendar until I reached magic number 99. With only 99 days left to go, I could call myself a "double digit midget". Short timers often became very nervous and paranoid as it was believed their odds of being injured or killed was very high. Everybody in camp was on edge that night because the massive enemy Tet offensive of 1968 had occurred a year earlier and it was feared another was coming. Sometime during the night, we began to hear a radio outside the camp playing Christmas songs. That was so strange since we always did a sweep through the area in front of our bunkers looking for anything that might indicate recent activity, but none were found. The new guys wanted to start firing at the sound, but I stopped them, saying if Charlie wanted to share the spirit of Christmas, stand down, be alert and ready, but enjoy the brief moment of peace. I was very nervous knowing someone, somehow had been able to take up a position we had searched just a few hours earlier very close to our location. Sometime later, the music stopped and nothing further happened. I learned later the Viet Cong had an underground tunnel system near our camp that extended partially beneath our camp area. One portion of the tunnel was used as a hospital facility for them, and this helped explain some of the mysterious sounds and sudden appearances and disappearances of VC, particularly at night. The famous "Tunnel Systems of Cu Chi" were found in our area of operations and are open today as a tourist attraction north of Saigon. Christmas day, we enjoyed a delicious traditional dinner with turkey, dressing and all the trimmings. Later that afternoon, we were allowed to make a radio-telephone call to our family back home that was very awkward because each time you finished a sentence, you had to say the phrase "over" in order for the radio operator to switch the call so the other party could speak. My parents never quite mastered the procedure, but we enjoyed a brief Christmas greeting. Christmas 1969 was in the books, and I was fast approaching my return to the "world".

CU CHI TUNNEL

THE FREEDOM FLIGHT HOME

February 22, 1970 I completed outbound processing at Long Bien Army Base and made my way over to Bien Hoa Airbase to catch the Freedom Bird. This time, roles were reversed from a year earlier and we were the veterans waiting for the newbies to arrive with our plane. They silently passed by us with wide eyes staring at how we looked after our year in Nam. We too remained silent, fearful something would happen to stop or delay our flight home, but as soon as the wheels of our World Airways Jet lifted off the runway, we exploded in a roar of excitement, knowing we were on our way home, standing tall and not in an aluminum casket! I made a mental note that the time of departure was 11:45 PM, February 22nd, 1969.

Our flight made one stopover in Tokyo, Japan and we flew non-stop after that until we landed in San Francisco for processing back into America through Oakland Army Base. When we deplaned on American soil, many, including me, got on all fours and kissed the tarmac. It was good to be alive and home! The time was 11:30 PM on February 22, 1970, 15 minutes before we began the flight due to our having crossed the International Date Line. In reality, the flight had taken almost 24 hours.

I had not slept in more than two days and was exhausted, still functioning on adrenaline. After arriving at Oakland, the first stop was at the base mess hall where we were greeted with friendly faces welcoming us back home and being treated to a grand, all you can eat steak dinner, our first in a very long time. Next, we headed to the showers for a hot bath, also a first in a long time, then we were issued new uniforms and shoes. Our old, filthy jungle fatigues, boots and underwear were taken out to be burned. After another long processing routine, we received our final pay, including airfare back home. Feeling clean again and on top of the world, filled with pride, we made our way back to San Francisco for the best ride yet, back home!

We knew the war had become very unpopular stateside, but we were not prepared for the reception we received. Some GIs changed into civilian clothes before leaving for the airport hoping they would not be recognized. Crowds of demonstrators, mostly hippie types, greeted us with jeers and cat calls, calling us baby killers. It continued throughout the airport. I did not expect cheering crowds, but I simply didn't know what to make of this reaction. Even the stewardess on the Delta flight to Atlanta was noticeably curt and disrespectful. After arriving in Atlanta and getting a good night's sleep in a real, clean bed, the first task was to purchase some civilian clothing and try to blend back into the local environment, hoping Vietnam was just a bad dream and would soon fade from memory, but that was not to be the case.

HOME AGAIN

Back home, I was welcomed by a few friends and family, retreated to my old bedroom and slept for what must have been a very long time. It felt good to be home, but I felt out of place, having survived in such a different world and having seen and done the things I was required to see and do. I felt different, with no one to relate to and not feeling comfortable after such a big change in environment in such a short time, with no adjustment period. I didn't want to talk to anyone or go anywhere, just hibernate. After more than a month of this behavior, just drifting with no direction in sight, my dad told me someone had left work at his bank, and he needed some extra help. I reluctantly agreed to begin helping temporarily and started work at the bank the next day, April 1st, 1970. I would spend the next 41 years of my life working there and it proved to be my salvation. It helped get me out into the public and push the memories of Vietnam into the back of my consciousness. Slowly I began to feel a sense of purpose and was able to crawl out of my shell.

FULFILLING THE PROMISE

I soon settled into the work and began to heal, feeling a sense of "belonging" again. I didn't care what I was paid, I was just enjoying the work. Thankfully I learned a lot during the next 2 ½ years, because I would soon need every bit of knowledge I had acquired when a very unexpected event took place. The evening of October 22, 1972, our family held a birthday party for my dad and his twin sister at the Springhill Country Club. Their 61st birthday would be the following day, October 23rd. During dinner that night, my dad suddenly collapsed onto the table. At that time, no 911 emergency service existed, so we carried him to the car and drove him to the emergency room at Tift General Hospital. The last physician he had seen was a young Internist in town named Dr. Bob Wight. Someone gave me his home telephone number and I called and asked him to come to the hospital, which he did immediately. It was a very long night and Dr. Wight finally came out to tell us my dad had sustained a massive brain hemorrhage with the prognosis not being good. The next day, one day after his 61st birthday, my dad passed away.

I was not prepared for what followed and the next few months were very trying. The business had to go on, and there was no time to grieve. I did not feel prepared, but I knew it was up to me to take over his affairs and step into his shoes for the family business to survive and help my mother since she had absolutely no idea of what to do, dad always took care of everything. At 27 years old, the weight of responsibility was very heavy and I spent many sleepless nights worried I couldn't meet the challenge, but I would not quit, and I would step up to meet the challenge head on. During the next 41 years, I guided the business to success beyond my dad's imagination. I am so proud that I was able to look after my mom and her financial needs and made sure she never went lacking for anything.

Going to work every day was fun and exciting, helping my community and neighbors thrive, making it possible for thousands of people to realize their dreams. I financed thousands of new homes at affordable rates, financed churches, farmers, small businesses, individuals, rich and not so rich. During those years, I often prayed that God would reveal the purpose of the promise he made known to me those many years ago in Vietnam, that he would use me for his purpose. I kept waiting for an answer so I could direct my energies toward that goal. The answer came to me 45 years later, after I had retired, and came to believe I would never know.

In the summer of 2016, I carried an item to be sold at auction in Lakeland, Georgia. While waiting for my equipment to sell, I started a casual conversation with the man standing next to me I had just met by chance. He soon revealed he was there to purchase equipment for his pecan operation. Since I own a small pecan orchard, we began to have a discussion about pecan production. I soon learned he had been very successful and was a very large grower, owning thousands of acres of pecan trees and had become the largest pecan nurseryman in the world. I asked him how he had been so successful. He stated he got his start as a young man by renting someone's orchard and grew his first crop. The crop was successful, but he had used all his money to grow the crop and didn't have enough left to harvest it. He applied for loans at several banks and was turned down each time. Someone then told him to see the young banker in Lenox because he might help. The young banker took a chance and loaned him $5,000.00, unsecured, to harvest his first crop. I couldn't believe what I was hearing and asked him if he remembered the young banker's name, to which he replied he thought it was Warren Robinson! It was a loan I had made decades earlier, never remembering it until that moment. He was shocked when I told him **I** was the young banker that made the loan that started his business. It was at this moment I realized God had just revealed the answer to my prayers for the last 45 years. He had guided my steps at every turn, fulfilling his plan for my life. I had been doing his will every day for the last 45 years without ever realizing what was now so obvious.

UNITS COMPRISING FIRST INFANTRY DIVISION IN VIETNAM

1. 1st Bn, 26th Infantry
2. 1st and 2nd Bns, 18th Infantry
3. 1st Bn, 16th Infantry (Mech) and 2nd Bn, 16th Infantry
4. 1st Bn, 2nd Infantry and 2nd Bn, (Mech), 2nd Infantry
5. 1st Engineer Bn
6. 1st Aviation Bn
7. 121st Signal Bn
8. 701st Maint. Bn
9. 1st and 2nd Bns, 28th Infantry
10. Support Command
11. 1st Sq, 4th Cavalry
12. 1st S and T Bn
13. 1st Bn, 5th Arty
14. 1st Medical Bn
15. 1st Bn, 7th Arty
16. 1st MP Company
17. 2nd Bn, 33rd Arty
18. 8th Bn, 6th Arty
19. Division Artillery
20. 1st Brigade
21. 2nd Brigade
22. 3rd Brigade
23. Hqs and Hqs Co., 1st Admin Company

In addition to the Big Red One Division patch worn on one shoulder, the individual unit crest was worn on the other. Each unit had its own unique history and traditions to uphold along with its unique crest and there was a healthy rivalry between the units. Each one wanted to claim they were the "badest", meanest troops in the Army. In the 1960s, smoking cigarettes was almost universal, especially in the armed forces and the Zippo cigarette lighter was considered the "top of the line". Smoking was actually encouraged at times. Whenever we finished some physical task, the person in charge usually announced we would take a 5 minute break and to "light em if you got em", meaning a cigarette. In order to keep our smokes dry, we carried them in an aluminum, waterproof box. I improvised a technique for smoking during a driving monsoon rain. I would prop my helmet in a forward position on my head which provided just enough space out of the rain to light and enjoy a smoke. Practically every soldier had his Zippo engraved with his name, his unit, and other items such as a map of Vietnam or some slogan etc. My Zippo was engraved as follows: "Yea though I walk through the valley of the shadow of death, I will fear no evil for I am the evilest SOB in the Valley!"

2nd Battalion. 28th Infantry

WARREN ROBINSON

DIVISION ARTILLERY

MORTAR IN ACTION

WHAT'S WORTH REMEMBERING

Not much about the Vietnam experience is worth remembering, although many of those who served there can never get it out of their thoughts. However, one very important thing we must never forget are the veterans who fought there and the Christ-like way they loved each other.

This next section is devoted to illustrating the love these men shared for one another. While every man who served deserves special recognition for their service, the 1st Infantry Division had seven men who not only served with pride and honor, but who exemplified a selfless love for their comrades that exceeded anything expected of a soldier. These men were awarded the Congressional Medal of Honor, the nation's highest military award. The enemy did not take their lives from them, they willingly gave them up for their fellow man. They did not lose their lives; instead, they gained eternal life with our Lord and Savior, Jesus Christ.

1ST INFANTRY DIVISION MEDAL OF HONOR RECIPIENTS VIETNAM

2ND LIEUTENANT HAROLD BASCOM DURHAM, JR.
(Pinky)

S econd Lieutenant Harold Bascom Durham, Jr., (pinky). Lt. Durham was born October 13th, 1942 in Rocky Mount, North Carolina and listed his hometown of record as Atlanta, Georgia. Durham joined the Army in Atlanta in 1964 and was serving with battery C, 6th Battalion, 15th

Artillery Regiment, 1ˢᵗ Infantry Division on October 17ᵗʰ, 1967. During a firefight that day in Vietnam, Durham repeatedly exposed himself to hostile fire in order to direct artillery bombardment, even after being severely wounded. He was killed during that battle and was posthumously awarded the Medal of Honor for his actions. His citation reads, "2ⁿᵈ Lieutenant Durham, Artillery, distinguished himself by conspicuous gallantry and intrepidity at the cost of his own life above and beyond the call of duty while assigned to Battery C. 2ⁿᵈ Lieutenant Durham was serving as a forward observer with Company D, 2ⁿᵈ Battalion, 28ᵗʰ Infantry during a battalion reconnaissance in force mission. At approximately 1015 hours, contact was made with an enemy force concealed in well-camouflaged positions and fortified bunkers. 2ⁿᵈ Lt. Durham immediately moved into an exposed position to adjust the supporting artillery fire onto the insurgents. During a brief lull in the battle he administered emergency first aid to the wounded in spite of heavy enemy sniper fire directed toward him. Moments later, as enemy units assaulted friendly positions, he learned that Company A, bearing the brunt of the attack, had lost its forward observer. While he was moving to replace the wounded observer, the enemy detonated a Claymore mine, severely wounding him in the head and impairing his vision. In spite of the intense pain, he continued to direct the supporting artillery fire and to be placed almost directly on his position. Twice the insurgents were driven back, leaving many dead and wounded behind. 2ⁿᵈ Lt. Durham was then taken to a secondary defensive position. Even in his extremely weakened condition, he continued to call artillery fire onto the enemy. He refused to seek cover and instead positioned himself in a small clearing which offered a better vantage point from which to adjust the fire. Suddenly, he was severely wounded a second time by enemy machine gun fire. As he lay on the ground near death, he saw two Viet Cong approaching, shooting defenseless wounded men. With his last effort, 2ⁿᵈ Lt. Durham shouted a warning to a nearby soldier who immediately killed the insurgents. 2ⁿᵈ Lt. Durham died moments later, still griping the radio handset. 2ⁿᵈ Lt. Durham's gallant actions in close combat with an enemy force are in keeping with the highest traditions of the military service and reflect great credit upon himself, his unit, and the U. S. Army.

2ⁿᵈ Lt. Durham, Pinky, grew up in Tifton, Georgia in a home with two other siblings, a brother and sister. He attended Tifton High School and graduated in 1960. His father was living in Colorado and was ailing, so he decided to relocate to Colorado Springs. He worked at the Broadmoor Hotel and attended A & M University. Then he decided to join the Army. He completed his first tour in Vietnam, came home and went to Officer Candidate School at Fort Sill, Oklahoma. He believed in what he was doing. After completing his schooling in 1967, he volunteered to replace the forward observer for Co. D, 2nd Infantry "Black Lions" Just 17 days into his second tour, he was killed in a search and destroy mission near Chon Thank. The battle was a slaughter leaving 58 dead, 2 Missing in Action and 75 wounded. Harold was awarded the Congressional Medal of Honor, Bronze Star w/Bronze V for valor and Valor Bronze Oak Cluster, Purple Heart, Army Commendation, Army Good Conduct, National Defense, Vietnam Service w/2 Bronze star, Vietnam campaign Medals and Vietnam Gallantry Cross Unit Citation. Lieutenant Durham was buried in Oakridge Cemetery in Tifton, Georgia.

2ND LIEUTENANT ROBERT J. HIBBS

Lieutenant Hibbs was born April 21st, 1943 in Omaha, Nebraska. He entered service at Des Moines, Iowa and was killed in action on March 5th, 1966 at Don Dien Lo Ke, Republic of Vietnam. Lt. Hibbs served in Company B, 2nd Battalion, 28th Infantry, 1st Infantry Division.

His Medal of Honor citation reads:

For conspicuous gallantry and intrepidity at the risk of life above and beyond the call of duty, 2nd Lt. Hibbs was in command of a 15-man ambush patrol of the 2nd Battalion, when his unit observed a company of Viet Cong advancing along the road toward the 2nd Battalion's position. Informing his command post by radio of the impending attack, he prepared his men for the oncoming Viet Cong, emplaced 2 mines in their path and, when the insurgents were within 20 feet of the patrol's position, he fired the 2 antipersonnel mines, wounding or killing half of the enemy company. Then, to cover the withdrawal of his patrol, he threw hand grenades, stepped onto the open road, and opened fire on the remainder of the Viet Cong force of approximately 50 men. Having rejoined his men, he was leading them toward the battalion perimeter when the patrol encountered the rear elements of another Viet Cong company deployed to attack the battalion. With the advantage of surprise, he directed a charge against the Viet Cong, which carried the patrol through the insurgent force, completely disrupting its attack. Learning that a wounded patrol member was wandering in the area between the 2 opposing forces and although moments from safety and wounded in the leg himself, he and a sergeant went back to the battlefield to recover the stricken man. After they grabbed the dazed soldier and dragged him back toward the friendly lines while 2nd Lieutenant Hibbs remained behind to provide covering fire. Armed with only an M-16 rifle and a pistol, but determined to destroy the enemy positions, he then charged the 2 machine gun emplacements and was struck down. Before succumbing to his mortal wounds, he destroyed the starlight telescope sight attached to his rifle to prevent its capture and use by the Viet Cong. 2nd Lieutenant Hibbs' profound concern for his fellow soldiers, and his intrepidity at the risk of his life above and beyond the call of duty ae in the highest traditions of the U. S. Army and reflect great credit upon himself and the Armed Forces of his country.

SERGEANT FIRST CLASS MATTHEW LEONARD

Sergeant Leonard was born November 26th, 1929 in Eutaw, Alabama and was killed in action on February 28th, 1967 at the age of 37. Sergeant Leonard served with the 16th Infantry Regiment, 1st Infantry Division and is buried in Fort Mitchell National Cemetery, Fort Mitchel,

Alabama. Sergeant Leonard's Medal of Honor was presented posthumously to Leonard's wife by President Lyndon B. Johnson during a ceremony at the Pentagon on December 19th, 1968. Sergeant Leonard served in both the Korean War as well as the War in Vietnam. His awards include the Medal of Honor, Purple Heart and Combat Infantryman badge, 2nd award. Sergeant Leonard's citation reads as follows:

"For conspicuous gallantry and intrepidity in actions at the risk of his life above and beyond the call of duty, his platoon was suddenly attacked by a large enemy force employing small arms, automatic weapons, and hand grenades. Although the platoon leader and several other key leaders were among the first wounded, Platoon Sergeant Leonard quickly rallied his men to throw back the initial enemy assaults. During the short pause that followed, he organized a defensive perimeter, redistributed ammunition, and inspired his comrades through his forceful leadership and words of encouragement. Noticing a wounded companion outside the perimeter, he dragged the man to safety but was struck by a sniper's bullet which shattered his left hand. Refusing medical attention and continuously exposing himself to the increasing fire as the enemy again assaulted the perimeter, Platoon Sergeant Leonard moved from position to position to direct the fire of his men against the well camouflaged foe. Under the cover of the main attack, the enemy moved a machine gun into a location where it could sweep the entire perimeter. This threat was magnified when the platoon machine gun in this area malfunctioned. Platoon Sergeant Leonard quickly crawled to the gun position and was helping to clear the malfunction when the gunner and other men in the vicinity were wounded by fire from the enemy machine gun. Platoon Sergeant Leonard rose to his feet, charged the enemy gun and destroyed the hostile crew despite being hit several times by enemy fire. He moved to a tree, propped himself against it, and continued to engage the enemy until he succumbed to his many wounds. His fighting spirit, heroic leadership, and valiant acts inspired the remaining members of his platoon to hold back the enemy until assistance arrived. Platoon Sergeant Leonard's profound courage and devotion to his men are in keeping with the highest traditions of the military service, and his gallant actions reflect great credit upon himself and the United States Army.

SERGEANT DONALD RUSSELL LONG

Sergeant Donald Russell Long was born August 27th, 1938 in Blackfork, Ohio and died at age 26 on June 30th, 1966 in Vietnam while serving with the 4th Cavalry Regiment of the 1st Infantry Division. He was buried in Union Baptist Church Cemetery in Blackfork, Ohio.

Long was of mixed race (Black, White and Native American). Many of his ancestors, along with a majority of the Blackfork community were descendants of free people from Virginia and North Carolina. Many of them were Native Americans from tribes such as the Saponi. Sergeant Long graduated from Decatur-Washington High School in Blackfork, Ohio and joined the army in Ashland, Kentucky in 1963. By June 30th, 1966 he was serving as a Sergeant in Troop C, 1st Squadron, 4th Cavalry Regiment of the 1st Infantry Division in Vietnam.

On that day, Long's unit came under heavy attack during a reconnaissance patrol. During the battle, a hand grenade was thrown near Long and the crew of a disabled armored personnel carrier. Long threw himself onto the grenade, successfully protecting his fellow soldiers while sacrificing his own life. His Medal of Honor citation follows:

"For conspicuous gallantry and intrepidity in action at the risk of his life above and beyond the call of duty. Troops B and C, while conducting a reconnaissance mission along a road were suddenly attacked by a Viet

Cong regiment, supported by mortars, recoilless rifles and machine guns, from concealed positions astride the road. Sergeant Long abandoned the relative safety of his armored personnel carrier and braved a withering hail of enemy fire to carry wounded men to evacuation helicopters. As the platoon fought it's way forward to resupply advanced elements, Sergeant Long repeatedly exposed himself to enemy fire at point blank range to provide the needed supplies. While assaulting the Viet Cong position, Sergeant Long inspired his comrades by fearlessly standing unprotected to repel the enemy with rifle fire and grenades as they attempted to mount his carrier. When the enemy threatened to overrun a disabled carrier nearby, Sergeant Long again disregarded his own safety to help the severely wounded crew to safety. As he was handing arms to the less seriously wounded and reorganizing them to press the attack, an enemy grenade was hurled onto the carrier deck. Immediately recognizing the imminent danger, he instinctively shouted a warning to the crew and pushed to safety one man who had not heard his warning over the roar of battle. Realizing that these actions would not fully protect the exposed crewmen from the deadly explosion, he threw himself over the grenade to absorb the blast and thereby saved the lives of 8 of his comrades at the expense of his own. Throughout the battle, Sergeant Long's extraordinary heroism, courage and supreme devotion to his men were in the finest tradition of the military service, and reflect great credit upon himself and the United States Army."

CAPTAIN EURIPIDES RUBIO

Captain Rubio was born March 1st, 1938 in Ponce, Puerto Rico. He died November 8th, 1966 at the age of 28 in Tay Ninh Province, Republic of Vietnam during Operation Attleboro and is buried in Puerto Rico National Cemetery in Bayamon, Puerto Rico. Captain Rubio served with Headquarters and Headquarters Company, 1st Battalion, 28th Infantry (Black Lions) of the 1st Infantry Division in Vietnam. Captain Rubio was one of nine Puerto Ricans who were awarded the United States' highest military decoration for valor, the Medal of Honor. He joined the Army at Fort Buchanan, Puerto Rico in 1956.

On November 8th, 1966, during Operation Attleboro in Tay Ninh Province, South Vietnam, Captain Rubio's company came under attack from the North Vietnamese Army; leaving the safety of his post, Captain Rubio received two serious wounds as he braved the intense enemy fire to distribute ammunition, re-establish positions and render aid to the wounded. Despite his pain, he assumed command when a rifle company commander was medically evacuated. He was then wounded a third time as he tried to move amongst his men to encourage them to fight with renewed effort.

While aiding the evacuation of wounded personnel, he noted that a US smoke grenade, which was intended to mark the Viet Cong's position for an air strike, had fallen dangerously close to friendly lines. He ran to move the grenade but was immediately struck to his knees by enemy fire. Despite his wounds, Captain Rubio managed to collect the grenade and again run through enemy fire to within 20 meters of the enemy position to throw the by-then already smoking grenade into the enemy before he fell for the final time. Using the now-repositioned grenade as a marker, friendly air strikes were directed to destroy the hostile positions.

Captain Rubio's singularly heroic act turned the tide of battle, and for his extraordinary leadership and valor, he posthumously received the Medal of Honor. His Medal of Honor Citation is as follows:

"For conspicuous gallantry and intrepidity in action at the risk of his life above and beyond the call of duty, Captain Rubio, Infantry, was serving as communications officer, 1ˢᵗ Battalion, when a numerically superior enemy force launched a massive attack against the battalion defense position. Intense enemy machine gun fire raked the area while mortar rounds and rifle grenades exploded within the perimeter. Leaving the relative safety of his post, Captain Rubio received 2 serious wounds as he braved the withering fire to go to the area of most intense action where he distributed ammunition, re-established positions and rendered aid to the wounded. Disregarding the painful wounds, he unhesitatingly assumed command when a rifle company commander was medically evacuated. Captain Rubio was wounded a third time as he selflessly exposed himself to the devastating enemy fire to move among his men to encourage them to fight with renewed effort. While aiding the evacuation of wounded personnel, he noted a smoke grenade which was intended to mark the Viet Cong position for air strikes had fallen dangerously close to the friendly lines. Captain Rubio ran to reposition the grenade but was immediately struck to his knees by enemy fire. Despite his several wounds, Captain Rubio scooped up the grenade, ran through the deadly hail of fire to within 20 meters of the enemy position and hurled the already smoking grenade into the midst of the enemy before he fell for the final time. Using the repositioned grenade as a marker, friendly air strikes were directed to destroy the hostile positions. Captain Rubio's singularly heroic bravery and selfless concern for his men are in keeping with the highest traditions of the military service and reflect great credit on Captain Rubio and the U.S. Army."

SERGEANT JAMES W. ROBINSON, JR. (JIM)

Sergeant Robinson was born August 30th, 1940 in Hinsdale, Illinois and died April 11th, 1966 at the age of 25 in Phuoc Tuy Province, Republic of Vietnam. He is buried in Clarendon Hills Cemetery in Darien, Illinois. Sergeant Robinson served in the Marine Corp from 1958 until 1961, then he joined the Army in 1964.

Born in 1940 in Hinsdale, Illinois, a Chicago suburb, Robinson graduated from Morton High School in 1958 and enlisted in the U. S. Marines, serving primarily in Okinawa. After his service ended in 1961, Robinson worked in the private sector in Northern Virginia, then re-enlisted in 1964, this time in the U. S. Army. Assigned to duty in Panama, Robinson relentlessly requested a transfer to Southeast Asia, which was finally granted in 1965. He was assigned to Company C, 2nd Battalion, 16th Infantry of the 1st Infantry Division. Robinson was the first Virginia resident to receive the Medal of Honor during the Vietnam War. His Medal of Honor Citation reads as follow:

"For conspicuous gallantry and intrepidity in action at the risk of his life above and beyond the call of duty. Company C was engaged in fierce combat with a Viet Cong battalion. Despite the heavy fire, Sergeant Robinson moved among the men of his fire team, instructing and inspiring them, and placing them in advantageous positions. Enemy snipers located in nearby trees were inflicting heavy casualties on forward elements of Sergeant Robinson's unit. Upon locating the enemy sniper whose fire was taking the heaviest toll, he took a grenade launcher and eliminated the sniper.

Seeing a medic hit while administering aid to a wounded sergeant in front of his position and aware that now the 2 wounded men were at the mercy of the enemy, he charged through a withering hail of fire and dragged his comrades to safety, where he rendered first aid and saved their lives. As the battle continued and casualties mounted, Sergeant Robinson moved about under intense fire to collect from the wounded their weapons and ammunition and redistribute them to able-bodied soldiers. Adding his fire to that of his men, he assisted in eliminating a major enemy threat.

Seeing another wounded comrade in front of his position, Sergeant Robinson again defied the enemy's fire to effect a rescue. In so doing he was himself wounded in the shoulder and leg. Despite his painful wounds, he dragged the soldier to shelter and saved his life by administering first aid. While patching his own wounds, he spotted an enemy machine gun which had inflicted a number of casualties on the American force. His rifle ammunition expended, he seized 2 grenades and, in an act of unsurpassed heroism, charged toward the entrenched enemy weapon. Hit again in the leg, this time with a tracer round which set fire to his clothing, Sergeant Robinson ripped the burning clothing from his body and staggered indomitably through the enemy fire, now concentrated solely on him, to within grenade range of the enemy machine gun position. Sustaining 2 additional chest wounds, he marshaled his fleeting strength and hurled the 2 grenades, thus destroying the enemy gun position, as he fell dead upon the battlefield.

His magnificent display of leadership and bravery saved several lives and inspired his soldiers to defeat the numerically superior enemy force. Sergeant Robinson's conspicuous gallantry and intrepidity, at the cost of his life, are in keeping with the finest traditions of the U. S. Army and reflect great credit upon the 1st Infantry Division and the U. S. Armed Forces."

SPECIALIST FOUR ROBERT F. STRYKER

Specialist Stryker was born November 9th, 1944 in Auburn, New York. He joined the Army at Throop, New York in 1963 and was killed in action November 7th, 1967 at the age of 22 at Binh Long, South Vietnam. Specialist Stryker served with Company C, 1st Battalion, 26th Infantry, 1st Infantry Division. He is buried in Pine Hill Cemetery in Throop, New York.

The Stryker combat vehicle is named in his and Private First Class Stuart S. Stryker's honor (no relation).

Specialist Strykers' Medal of Honor Citation reads as follows:

"For conspicuous gallantry and intrepidity at the risk of his life above and beyond the call of duty. Specialist Stryker, U.S. Army, distinguished himself while serving with Company C. Stryker was serving as a grenadier in a multicompany reconnaissance in force near Loc Ninh. As his unit moved through the dense underbrush, it was suddenly met with a hail of rocket, automatic weapons and small arms fire from enemy forces concealed in fortified bunkers and in the surrounding trees. Reacting quickly, Specialist Stryker fired into the enemy positions with his grenade launcher. During the devastating exchange of fire, Specialist Stryker detected enemy elements attempting to encircle his company and isolate it from the main body of the friendly force. Undaunted by the enemy machine gun and small arms fire, Specialist Stryker repeatedly fired grenades into the trees, killing enemy snipers and enabling his comrades to sever the attempted encirclement. As the battle continued, Specialist Stryker observed several wounded members of his squad in the killing zone of an enemy claymore mine. With complete disregard for his surroundings, he tripped and landed himself upon the mine as it was detonated. He was mortally wounded as his body absorbed the blast and shielded his comrades from the explosion. His unselfish actions were responsible for saving the lives of at least 6 of his fellow soldiers. Specialist Stryker's great personal bravery was in keeping with the highest traditions of the military service and reflects great credit upon himself, his unit, and the U. S. Army."

EPILOGUE

I n the midst of deafening noise, terror, screams of pain from the dead and dying, when the natural inborn reaction is for self-survival, countless individuals pushed those things to the side and sprang forward into the mist of the holocaust to save and protect the fallen, without regard for their personal safety. It seems to defy all logic. But they were driven to these heights of courage by the most powerful force in the universe, love. The brotherly love shared by the combat soldier of all wars which they alone will ever know.

No one could have predicted these seemingly ordinary kids possessed the inner strength or wherewithal to ever be capable of such exceptional heroism. The examples recorded in this book are only a glimpse of the countless acts of selflessness and brotherly love Jesus himself first demonstrated on the cross of Calvary.

Where do these men come from and how does America continue to produce the extraordinary men and women who are willing to lay down their own life for the good of their country and their fellow man? The author does not pretend to have an answer for this question, but the answer lies somewhere in our Christian heritage as Americans. Love and only love can motivate ordinary men to these extraordinary heights of courage.

In the decades since our war was over, a grateful nation has at last recognized our service and welcomed us home with honor and respect. We loved each other so much we would lay down our lives for our comrades; however, the greatest challenge remains before us, and that is to let go of the guilt we carry with us each day as survivors and learn to love and forgive ourselves.

VIETNAM STATISTICAL PROFILE OF WARRIORS IN COUNTRY AND IN UNIFORM STATISTICS EXTRACTED FROM THE DEFENSE CASUALTY ANALYSIS SYSTEM AS OF APRIL 29, 2008

Casualty Category	Number of Records
Accident	9,107
Declared Dead	1,201
Died of Wounds	5,299
Homicide	236
Illness	938
Killed in Action	40,934
Presumed Dead (Body Remains Recovered	32
Presumed Dead (Body Remains not Recovered)	91
Self Inflicted	382
Total Records	58,220

Country of Casualty

Laos	728
Cambodia	523
China	10
North Vietnam	1,120
South Vietnam	55,661
Thailand	178
Total Records	58,220

Home state of Record

Alabama	1,208
Alaska	57
American Samoa	4
Arizona	619
Arkansas	592
California	5,575
Canal Zone	2
Colorado	623
Connecticut	612
Delaware	122
District of Columbia	242
Florida	1,654
Foreign	4
Georgia	1,581
Guam	70
Hawaii	276
Idaho	217
Illinois	2,936
Indiana	1,534
Iowa	851

Kansas	627
Kentucky	1,056
Louisiana	885
Maine	341
Maryland	1,014
Massachusetts	1,331
Michigan	2,657
Minnesota	1,077
Mississippi	636
Missouri	1,418
Montana	267
Nebraska	396
Nevada	149
New Hampshire	226
New Jersey	1,487
New Mexico	395
New York	4,119
North Carolina	1,613
North Dakota	199
Ohio	3,094
Oklahoma	987
Oregon	710
Pennsylvania	3,147
Puerto Rico	345
Rhode Island	209
South Carolina	895
South Dakota	192
Tennessee	
Texas	3,415
Utah	361
Vermont	100
Virgin Islands	15
Virginia	1,305

West Virginia	733
Wyoming	119
Total Records	58,220

Hostile or Non Hostile Death

Hostile Death	47,434
Non Hostile Death	10,786
Total Records	58,220

Year of Death

1956-1959	4
1960	5
1961	16
1962	53
1963	122
1964	216
1965	1,928
1966	6,350
1967	11,363
1968	16,899
1969	11,780
1970	6,173
1971	2,414
1972	759
1973	68
1974	1
1975	62
1976-1979	0
1980-1986	0
1987	1

1988–1989	0
1990	1
1991–1999	0
2000–2006	5
Total Records	58,220

Gender

Male	58,212
Female	8
Total	58,220

Service Component

National Guard	97
Regular	34,508
Reserve	5,762
Selective Service	17,671
Not Reported	182
Total	58,220

Pay Grade

Enlistee (Grade E1-E9)	48,717
Officers (Grade O01-O08)	6,604
Warrant Officers (Grade Wo1-W04)	1,277
Undefined Code	1,622
Total	58,220

Service

Air Force	2,588
Army	38,224
Coast Guard	7
Marine Corps	14,844
Navy	2,559
Total	58,220

Race

American Indian	226
Asian	139
Black or African American	7,243
Hispanic	349
Native Hawaiian or Pacific Islander	229
Non Hispanic	204
White	49,830
Total	58,220

Religion

Assemblies of God	117
Baptist	9,484
Brethren Churches	63
Buddhism	53
Christian Church	34
Christian, No Denomination	1
Church of Christ	528
Church of God	238
Church of Jesus Christ of Latter Day Saints (Mormon)	589

Church of the Nazarene	132
Congregational Churches	1
Episcopal Church	825
First Church of Christ, Scientist (Christian Science)	63
Friends (Quakers)	12
Islam	12
Jehova's Witness	26
Judaism (Jewish)	270
Lutheran	2,253
Methodist Churches	4,077
No Religious Preference	3,106
Pentecostal Church (USA)	182
Presbyterian Church (USA)	1,303
Protestant, No Denominational Preference	16,647
Protestant, Other Churches	558
Reformed Church in America	45
Roman Catholic Church	16,818
Seventh Day Adventist	116
Southern Baptist Convention	121
Unclassified Religions	487
United Church of Christ	11
Total	58,220

1ˢᵀ INFANTRY DIVISION CASUALTIES

May 1967 – December 1967

You may not know anyone on this list, but each one named here was somebody's son, brother, father, friend or husband. They went to war as young men full of hope, plans and dreams for their future. Each one was special and deserves to be remembered for what they did. They will forever remain young in the minds of their loved ones and comrades. We will always remember them for what they did and for how much they loved us.

Acree, Roger L.

Adkins, Donald W.

Amos, Joe

Anderson, Larry M.

Anderson, William E.

Barker, Gary L.

Barnett, Billy Joe

Barr, Wilma J.

Beek, Irwin

Bermudez-Pacheco, E.

Blackburn, Jerry E.

Boger, Rhine H.

Booker, Joseph O.

Adams, Ronald M.

Allen, Terry De La

Amos, William L.

Anderson, Richard A.

Banks, Larry C.

Barkley, Lawrence W.

Barnett, Glendon R.

Batchelor, Max W.

Benjamin, Kenneth R.

Biondillo, John C.

Blackwell, James L.

Bolen, Jackie Jr.

Brantlehy, John A.

Breeden, Clifford L.

Brown, Charles N.

Brown, Gregory L.

Brown, Richard G.

Bunyea, Walter C., Jr.

Burns, James L.

Carle, Gary L.

Carrasco, Ralph

Cederstrom, David O.

Chaney, Elwood D.

Chestnut, Gerry G.

Clayton, George D.

Cochran, Michael D.

Cook, Jerry

Cossa, William E.

Creason, Richard E.

Cross, Hugh W.

Cruz, Sam

Daily, Thomas B.

Davey, Glen V.

De Butts, Daniel F.

Denney, Alan W.

Denney, Alan W.

Dingle, Earl

Dossett, James E.

Dresher, Harry E., Jr.

Duffy, Lawrence R.

Durham, Harold B., Jr.

Dykema, Ross A.

Edenfield, Ronald D.

Ellis, Maurice S.

Enderiz, Victor A.

Ernst, Gary J.

Brickhouse, Emanuel

Brown, George M.

Brown, James R.

Brown, Walter

Burdett, Larry W.

Cable, Richard A.

Carpenter, Kenneth

Carter, Hubert C.

Chambers, Robert S.

Charlton, Jerry D.

Chriscoe, Charles R.

Clinger, Guy W., Jr.

Cole, William N.

Cook, Melvin B.

Courtney, James L.

Crites, Richard L.

Crutcher, Joe A.

Culvey, Kenneth L.

Daves, Donald C.

Davis, Willie L.

De Waal, Howard J.

Dessele, Richard J.

Desselle, Richard J.

Dodson, Wesley E.

Dowling, Frances E.

Dufford, Paul E.

Dunn, Lessell Jr.

Dye, Edward P.

East, Leon N.

Elchert, James M.

Elza, Ronald L.

Ensell, John R.

Evans, John R.

Familiare, Anthony

Farrell, Mitchell J.

Ferguson, Merle W.

Flansaas, Daniel R.

Foster, Larry R.

Friesner, Roger H.

Gallagher, Michael

Gandolfo, Philip N.

Garcia, Melleso

Gay, John B.

Gentry, Robert L.

Giacobello, Frank A.

Gilbertson, Verland

Gilpson, Gaylon

Greetan, Roger W.

Gribble, Ray N.

Gutierrez, Juan F.

Hamilton, James V.

Hancock, Edward D.

Hanno, Martin L.

Harris, Michael R.

Haskins, John M.

Haynes, John O.

Hendricks, Terry A.

Heyer, Edward E.

Hines, William J.

Holm, Donald H.

Holmes, Sammy L.

Horlbrack, Francis D.

Hutchison, Stanley

Igoe, William J.

Jagielo, Allen D.

Jett, William H.

Farhat, Alan J.

Feehery, Richard J.

Fisher, Henry I.

Foreman, Bobby L.

Fowler, Will L. D.

Fugua, Robert L., Jr.

Gamble, James H.

Garcia, Arturo

Gascon, Gary L.

Gazar, Guillermo

Gerstell, Howard M.

Gilbert, Stanley D.

Giovanacc, Richard

Goelz, Edward C.

Gretencord, Dean L.

Crissom, Gary L.

Hahn, Jeffrey C.

Hamlin, William L.

Hanno, Martin L.

Hanson, Kenneth G.

Harris, Robert T.

Hass, Stephen C.

Healey, Joseph

Hendrix, Kenneth L.

Hilton, David L.

Holleder, Donald W.

Holmes, John H.

Hook, Charles W.

Howard, David L.

Huyley, William D.

Irizarry-Hernandez

Jenkins, Lewis F.

Johnson, Cark T.

Johnson, Jerome

Jones, Michael A.

Jones, Thomas S.

Kelly, Charles P.

Kenter, Michael W.

Kerr, Stanley J.

Koschal, Gregory A.

Krische, John D.

Kurz, John P.

Lancaster, Jerry D.

Langham, Henry Jr.

Lee, Johnny A.

Lincoln, Gary G.

Logan, Douglas A.

Lopez, Jost

Luberda, Andrew P.

Lupo, Joseph C.

Mackey, Vertis L.

Malczynski, Matthew

McAndrew, Richard

McPherson, Staley

Megiveron, Emil G.

Metchlf, Larry D.

Miller, Michael M.

Morgan, Theodore Jr.

Morrow, Michael J.

Mucha, Howard A.

Murphy, Alfred W.

Myers, George L.

Natoli, Joseph R.

Noggle, Stephen M.

Nye, Wallace G.

O'Nail, Robert P.

Johnson, Willie C. J.

Jones, Richard W.

Jordan, Jerry K.

Kelly, Paul E., Jr.

Keppler, John M.

Knowlton, George F.

Kovanda, John M.

Kurtz, Robert W.

Lambert, Fred D.

Lange, Hans Dietric

Larson, James E.

Legere, Emile J.

Locke, George W., Jr.

Long, Charles E.

Lovato, Joe Jr.

Lucas, John W.

Lyons, James E.

Maguire, Robert S.

May, John A.

McClary, Gordon S.

McFalls, Billy C.

Meloy, Larry J.

Meyers, David L.

Minton, Bobby

Morrison, John F., Jr.

Moultrie, Joe D.

Muller, James V.

Murray, Thomas E.

Nagy, Robert J.

Nelson, Leroy A.

Nore, Kenneth H.

Nyman, Michael S.

Oestreicher, Paul A.

Oliver, Carl W.

Owens, Walter A.

Patterson, Dwayne M.

Peterson, Wayne A.

Platosz, Walter

Plotts, Richard

Poolaw, Pascal C., Sr.

Porter, Archie A.

Pays, Robert W.

Quinn, Daniel

Randall, Garland J.

Ray, John M.

Reed, Leroy

Reilly, Allan V.

Ribera, Antonio

Rieck, John J., Jr.

Robinson, Floyd I.

Romo, Francis

Roush, Robert R.

Sarsfield, Harry C.

Schneider, Terrance

Schrenk, Donald G.

Scott, David L.

Seadorf, Michael J.

Shegog, Willie L.

Sievers, Dale G., Jr.

Sikorski, Daniel

Smith, Edward A.

Snook, James A.

Sparks, James E.

Stanley, David C.

Starns, Dan C., Jr.

Steverson, Sim S.

Ostroff, Steven L.

Parker, Wesley

Payne, Ronald H.

Phillips, Ernest

Plier, Eugene J.

Poltkin, Martin L.

Pope, James E.

Porter, Joseph S., Jr.

Puckett, Troy M.

Rafferty, Edward J.

Ratcliffe, Carl Jr.

Reece, Ronney D.

Reed, Phillip E.

Remedies, Richard J.

Richards, Donald L.

Rivera, Trinidad NE

Roese, Alan

Rose, Barnes W., Jr.

Salvo, Joseph M.

Sauler. Charlie F.

Schramel, Kenneth M.

Schroder, Jack W.

Scriven, Samuel T.

Shaw, Clarence L.

Shubert, Jackie E.

Sikon, Robert A.

Simms, Leon

Smith, Luther A.

Sosa, Victoriano P.

Stallings, Ronald G.

Starks, James E.

Stephenson, William

Stigall, Arthur D.

Stoltenow, Ronald G.

Strizzi, Phillip A.

Sturdy, Alan M.

Tate, Kenneth W.

Thomas, Theodore D.

Thompson, Robert E.

Tizzio, Pasquale T.

Trantham, Van V., III

Tuholski, Gregory A.

Van Hoosier, James

Viggiano, Robert E.

Wagner, Roy C.

Warren, James R., Jr.

Wehreim, Richard J.

aWholford Lloyd

Wilson, Kenneth

Wiltse, James B., Jr.

Wissman, Ronald E.

Young, Harold E.

Stout, John H.

Stryker, Robert F.

Suggs, James D.

Thiel, John E.

Thompson, Otis F.

Tiller, Walter L.

Tomlinson, James H.

Tschumi, William J.

Turner, Larry E.

Verlinden, Craig A.

Villarreal, Johnny

Wallin, Douglas D.

Washungton, James E.

Wenderoth, Gerald

Williamson, Paul D.

Wilson, Sylvester, W.

Wing, Robert C.

Yancey, Joseph S.

Young, John E.

1ˢᵀ INFANTRY DIVISION CASUALTIES KILLED IN ACTION

January 1968 – December 1968

Abbie, Donald P.

Adams, George G.

Adcock, Billy A.

Alameda, William K.

Albert, Raymond H. J.

BAlbritton, Kenneth H.

Alles, James K.

Alongi, Michael P.J.

Anderson, Andrew C.

Anderson, Franklin

Anderson, Michael N.

Arenas, Manuel V., Jr.

Aronce, Joseph C.

Austin, William O.

Azore, David

Bailey, Flord C.

Baker, Philip K.

Bandy, Michael J.

Barbery, Robert N.

Bartkowski, Gregory

Abbott, Edward

Adams. Jesse L.

Ake, Homer l., Jr.

Albanese, Luigi F.

Alberts, Roger D.

Allen, Donald W., Jr.

Allison, James S.

Ambrose, Gregory F.

Anderson, David A.

Anderson, James A.

Anderson, Roy L.

Arens, Reynaldo

Asato, Wallace S.

Avery, Ronnie G.

Babiarz, Edward M.

Baker, Jerald L.

Baldwin, Michael R.

Baney, William G., Jr.

Bartell, Larry M.

Bates, Wayne S.

Bayonet, Thomas W.

Beatty, Leonard Jr.

Bechard, John C.

Becker, Thomas L.

Bell, Homer B.

Bennett, Howard D.

Bertsch, Brent J.

Best, Ronald L.

Bishop, Thomas W.

Black, Harvey

Blacksten, Billy J.

Blauwkamp, Arlyn J.

Blume, Gerund J., Jr.

Bogart, Charles R.

Bond, Lawrence F.

Boots, Curtis E.

Borman, Jeradl A.

Bowman, Lester E., Jr.

Boyle, James P.

Brannon, Walter L.

Brenner, David A.

Brockman, John N.

Brophy, Martin E.

Brown, Hugh B., III

Brown, Rex L.

Brown, Richard A.

Brown, Thal A.

Bryan, Dan E.

Burgos,-Cruzadad, Ang

Burnam, Steven W.

Burnside, Donald R.

Burton, Thomas

Campos, Michael W.

Beard, Charles C.

Becannen, Barry J.

Beck, Steven L.

Behm, Stanley W.

Belletti, Anthony J.

Berg, Ray W., Jr.

Bess, Benny D.

Betts, Terry W.

Bitel, Ben S.

Black, Ralph R.

Bland, Isaac

Bloyer, Sheldon E.

Boehm, Bradley W.

Bolton, David J.

Bonifant, Samuel H.

Boots, James A.

Bowen, Larry W.

Boyce, Eugene R.

Bradley, Martee, Jr.

Breitnitz, Lawrence

Brock, James B.

Brooks, James L.

Brown, Dierothen

Brown, Raymond L.

Brown, Richard C.

Brown, Ronald L.

Browne, Gordon F.

Buchanan, Gilbert E.

Burleson, John A.

Burnsed, Randell H.

Burrows, Marvin E.

Callwood, Gladston

Cannon, Robert E.

Carmody, Jan A.

Carson, Edwin E.

Carter, Thiul G., III

Caswell, Raymond

Catt, Joseph F.

Chambers, Udell

Chilton, Richard K.

Christensen, Dick

Ciupinski, James M.

Clark, Kendell H.

Clayton, Benny D.

Coates, James R.

Cobb, Raymond

Cohn, William P., Jr.

Cole, Robert L.

Collins, James G.

Colon-Perez, Abraha

Compton, Lorn D.

Connolly, Thomas C.

Cook, Charles J.

Cooper, Willie G.

Cornell, Ricky L.

Cosgriff, Paul L.

Cottrell, Timothy J.

Courtney, Ronnie

Covington, Rory A.

Coy, Jessie E. L.

Crabtree, Varise H.

Crook, James P.

Crosby, Robert M.

Cuellar, Pilay J.

Curtis, Herber R.

Czerwonka, August E.

Carroll, Patriek J.

Carter, Hamp, Jr.

Cassidy, David A

Cates, Robert M., Jr.

Cavis, David J.

Chilcote, Bryan M.

Christensen, Alvin

Christy, Richard T.

Clark, Douglas M.

Clarke, William V.

Cleem, Larry L.

Coaxum, Theodore

Coggins, James T.

Cole, Billy J.

Collins, Arlin D.

Collins, Mark P.

Compton, Johnnie R.

Connclly, Samuel G.

Connors, David T.

Cooper, James E.

Coppo, Patrick B.

Cornwell, Harry J.

Costin, Charles G.

Coulon, John G.

Covington, Claude H.

Cox, Everett F.

Coyle, Gerald

Cronin, David M.

Cropper, Ray D.

Cudworth, Albert W.

Curley, Raymon N.

Cysewski, Gary F.

Dameron, Robert W.

Dargan, Jeffrey L.

Davis Ernest P.

Davis, Roland K.

De Jeus-Munuz, Ale

Dtan, Glenn F.

Deeter, David K.

Dengler, John L.

Derrick, Randy W.

Direen, Kevin T.

Dominguez, Frank L.

Downing, Michael W.

Draper, William M.

Durst, John B.

Dyer, Willford L.

Eichenauer, Thomas

Elmandorf, Arthur D.

Evans, Clarence L.

Evans, Lloyd W., Jr.

Falardeav, Joseph E.

Fellshaw, John A.

Fernandez, Gary

Figueroa, Albert

Fix, Michael D.

Fox, Charles B., Jr.

Franks, Joseph R.

Frechette, Thrry A.

Friedhoff, Dennis P.

Gabel, Gary L.

Gamelin, Ernet V.

Garth, Clyde Jr.

Gershnow, Steven A.

Gibis, Michael E.

Gifford, Robert A.

Darling, Larry W.

Davis, John W.

Davis, Steven F.

De Marr, John C.

Debo, William L.

Deleon, Herman B.

Denton, David A.

Dillow, Keven T.

Doan, Lester A.

Douglas, Johnnie L.

Drake, Roger K.

Dugan, Kevin

Dutrol, Richard 'T.

Efird, Franklin O. D.

Eldridge, William F.

Elswick, Robert W.

Evans, Joe F.

Ezell, Burey D.

Fazzino, James D.

Ferguson, James A.

Fetter, Kenneth L.

Fitzimmons, Larry L.

Flohr, George

Fox, Robert L., JR.

Fray, Earl R.

Freestone, Spencer

Gabana, Roberto L.

Galata, John M.

Garcia, Joseph A.

Gercz, Francis G., Jr.

Geyer, Leroy C.

Gibson, David

Giles, Clem C.

Gill, Joseph G.

Gilsinger, Frederic

Goldberg, Benjamin

Gomez-Rivera, Juan

Gonzalez, Velez Joe

Gorham, Marc C.

Graham, Charles W.

Graves, James E.

Green, David H., Jr.

Green, Melvin R.

Gregory, Philip L.

Griggs, Harvey F.

Guerra-Hernandez, R.

Guley, David A.

Gutierrez, Jose D.

Haas, Frederick W.

Haley, Jerry R.

Hall, George M.

Hamby, Jimmy W.

Hammond, Charles W.

Hampshire, Robert C.

Hansen, John M.

Hanson, Stephen M.

Harmon, Carey D.

Harrington, Hugh L.

Harris, Gary B.

Harris, Jimmy L.

Hay, James S.

Hayes, Quentin

Hebert, Milvin D.

Heggan, Donald E.

Hellenbrand, David

Herndon, Donald L.

Gillespie, Robert J.

Godwin, James R.

Golden, Jack D.

Gonzales, Vincent

Goode, Jack D.

Gottwald, George J.

Granados, Richard

Gray, Gregory V.

Green, Jeffery W.

Greendyke, Gerald R.

Greiner, Donald H.

Gruber, Martin S., Jr.

Guillen, Phillip O.

Gulie, James P.

Guy, Allen E.

Hagan, Robert A., Jr.

Hall, Chauncey J.

Halverson, Gary J.

Hammer, Robert W.

Hammond, Gerald, Jr.

Hankison, Tommy L.

Hansen, Stephen M.

Hanson, William H.

Harrell, Lovett L.

Harris, Ervin E.

Harris, Grady H.

Hartpence, Dennis R.

Hayes, Christopher

Hayes, Thomas J., IV

Hederman, Patrick S.

Heissenbuttel, Pete

Henson, Gwyn T.

Herrera, Jose B.

Herron, Dennis

Hicks, Jeffrey L.

Hill, Gary

Hill, Richard A.

Hilte, Frank E.

Hinkle Therry R.

Hinther, Gary B.

Hoffman, Ronnie J.

Holcomb, Daniel

Holmes, Norman W.

Horsley, Richard W.

Hough, Michael P.

Huffman, Eddie G.

Hughes, Sam Z.

Hutcherson, Gary C.

Jacobs, Aubrey E., Jr.

James, Billie

Jasper, David C.

Jenkins, Wayne D.

Jirsa, Peter J.

Johnson, Byron, S.

Johnson, Haywood, Jr.

Johnson, Samuel, Jr.

Johnson, William W.

Jones, Freddie L.

Jones, Jimmie D.

Jones, Stephen C.

Jordan, James E., Jr.

Kame, William G.

Keels, Marlowe E.

Kennedy, John F.

Keyes, William G.

Kimbley, Robert G.

Hertel, Rodger R.

Hill, Dale A.

Hill, James W.

Hilley, Robert L.

Hilyard, James H.

Hinnant, Benjamin L.

Hodges, Robert G.

Holbrook, Jefferey

Holland, Wayne B.

Holtz, Alfred J., Jr.

Houcharoff, Gene E.

Hudson, George A., Jr.

Hughes, Billy E. H.

Humphrey, Johnny W.

Jackson, Lamont

Jaime, Antonio B.

Jarrard, Jerry E.

Jednat, Eric J.

Jessiman, Thad B.

Johnson, Barton W.

Johnson, David A.

Johnson, James G.

Johnson, Willard W.

Jones, Clifford R. J.

Jones, Henry, Jr.

Jones, Marrin H., Jr.

Jones, Thomas H.

Jurek, Edward J., II

Kardash, Kenneth M.

Kennedy, James

Kertis, Henry L.

Kimball, Pierce M.

Kindle, William D.

King, Kenneth W.

Kizer, Carl S.

Klose, Douglas C.

Knapper, Edward W.

Knouse, David W.

Koebke, John L.

Kolka, Edward L.

Kramer, Raymond L.

Krussow, Donald J.

Kyzer, Raymond B.

Lackey, Phillip L.

Laine, Wayne K.

Landers, Edmond J.

Lang, Dean L.

Laskowski, Anthony

Law, William L.

Le Fevre, Brian F.

Lee, Calvin R.

Lee, James R.

Lemay, Richard D., Jr.

Letendren, Richard

Levy, Bruce

Lewis, Donald G.

Licea, Francisco X.

Linder, John M.

Lockwood, Harold S.

Lozano, Donald J.

Luca, Allen L.

Lulla, Robert A.

Lyon, Christopher E.

Makuh, Frank J.

Macroscher, Albert G.

Martin, James E.

Kirkendoll, Cleeand

Klein, Michael K.

Knack, Richard C.

Knight, Carlos L.

Koch, Richard L.

Kohlbeck, Terrance

Koster, John K.

Kratzberg, Jimmie L.

Kuchek, Richard M.

La France, Jon P.

Lahti, James W.

Laird, Patrick S.

Landon, Gary J.

Lanier, Raymond E.

Latsch, David R.

Lawson, Thomas, Jr.

Ledbetter, Roger D.

Lee, Guy E.

Leisure, Jackie G.

Leonard, Sidney L.

Levinthol, John, Jr.

Lewis, Bobby D.

Libby, John H.

Likkel, Duane A.

Lockhard, David L.

Lopez, Miguel A.

Lozier, William E.

Lucisano, Rocco R.

Lutes, Mark S.

Makin, James B. L.

Manos, Arthur

Martin, Gerald

Martin, James L.

Martin, Kenneth L.

Martin, Ronald S.

Martin, William G.

Mason, Earnest L., Jr.

Matlock, John P.

McAfee, Cary F.

McCubbins, Larry J.

McDonald, Dennis E.

McNear, Terry L.

McCaskill, Fredric

Meldahl, Allen R.

Mendiola, Robert L.

Menz, Clyde R.

Meyer, Terry R.

Miller, Dennis J.

Miller, Glenn R.

Miller, Marvin I.

Mills, Richard T.

Mink, Boyd C.

Mitchell, Stephen

Mobley, Jenies I

Monroe, Marvin E.

Moore, Charles E., Jr.

Moore, Terry L.

Moorehouse, David L.

Morgan, Jackie M.

Muhich, Craig S.

Mullins, Earnest R.

Narvaez, Marrero

Noden, Timothy J.

Norris, James R.

North, Dale E.

O'connor, Mortimer

Martin, Lonnie G.

Martin, Thomas C.

Martinez, Juan P.

Mathers, Steven A.

Matlock, McKenley

McBurrows, Wendell

McDonald, Jerry V.

McIntire, Harman L.

McPheters, Chet E.

Meho, Jesus Q.

Mello, Edward T., Jr.

Mensch, Charles R.

Meyer, Leo R.

Milledge, Fredrick

Miller, Earnest L.

Miller, Hubert W.

Millhouse, Kenneth

Milstead, Antonio

Miskimmon, Johnathan

Mitchell, Thomas A.

Mocker, William F.

Montemayor, Jose S.

Moore, James C.

Mora, James J.

Moreno, Adolfa V.

Moss, Charles L., Jr.

Mulholland, Arnold

Nagelkirk, Dennis P.

Neal, Kenneth L.

Nordstrom, Victor C.

Nortan, Dale E.

Northcutt, Danny R.

Oakes, Jack W.

Ohlson, Gallen E.

Okumura, Earl A.

Oliver, Henry M.

Oltman, Dean W.

Oquendo, Gutierrez

Ortega, Hilberto

Ouillette, Thomas R.

Owens, George A.

Oxner, Marion L.

Palm, Dale A.

Patrizio, Charles J.

Pederson, Dennis I.

Pellegrino, John P.

Perdue, George E.

Perry, Claude

Perry, Karl F.

Peters, Wilbert

Peterson, Russell G.

Pettie, Floyd W., III

Picard, Michael W.

Plummer, Richard E.

Pointer, Darryl W. A.

Ponath, Kurt F.

Pool, Gary G.

Potts, Wilmer

Price, Arnold W.

Propson, Marvin N.

Rades, Robert R.

Ramirez, Louis J.

Randolph, William J.

Reilly, John T.

Renteria, Rudolph S.

Reynolds, Michael M.

Okemah, John

Oleson, Joseph, Jr.

Olson, Alfred R

Omstead, David K.

Orem, Allen W.

Ortiz, Pedro M.

Oveton, Danny, Jr.

Owens, Larry T.

Pall, John J.

Paphe, Theodore A.

Peck, Jeffrey L.

Peina, Ernest D.

Pelletier, Paul J.

Permaloff, Charles

Perry, John E.

Peters, Albert J.

Petersen, Harry

Petraglia, Angco A.

Philbeck, Donald D.

Piper, Thomas L.

Plunkett, Gerald W.

Polisky, Thomas R.

Pool, Charles L.

Pooler, John S.

Pranger, Glenn A.

Price, Robert G.

Quick, Robert G.

Raines, Christopher

Randall, Michael A.

Reid, Ralph H.

Reno, Lawrence G.

Renville, Arden K.

Rhodes, Curtis A.

Ribucan, Van V.

Richards, Robert

Rivera-Galorza, B.

Rodriguez, Ramon S.

Rogers, William L.

Romero, Robert A.

Rouse, Frederick E.

Ruiz, John F.

Ruminski, Philipe

Russek, John J.

Ryan, Bernard S.

Salisbury, Gary E.

Sanchez, Rey8naldo A.

Sanzoverino, Willia

Sartor, Leonda

Schell, Randy S.

Schmale, William O.

Schramm, William G.

Schultz, James R.

Scott, Marvin

Scott, Sammy L.

Segura, Maxuel T.

Senne, Thomas A.

Settlemeyer, Jeffery

Sferruzzi, William

Shannon, Leroy, Jr.

Sheffield, Earnest

Sherman, Roosevelt

Shields, David T.

Shutters, Patrick A.

Siekierka, Donald B.

Simmons, Isiah

Singleton, Thomas A.

Rich, Craig A.

Riddick, Sterling G.

Robinson, Joseph B.

Rogers, Kenneth L.

Romano, Michael

Ross, Luther, Jr.

Rowland, Thomas W.

Rule, Ted T.

Rupert, John M.

Rutledge, James B.

Rygg, Charles A.

Samples, Stephen H.

Sandvig, Vernon D.

Sapp, Benny J.

Scales, Douglas

Schlinger, James I.

Schorndorf, Kenneth

Schultz, David C.

Scott, James G.

Scott, Michael J.

Sebens, Gaylord J.

Seltzer, Jackie R.

Serio, Robert F.

Sexton, Wayne E.

Shafer, William E.

Sheets, Orville A.

Shell, John R.

Sherrod, Walter, Jr.

Shirley, Harold G.

Sibley, Ralph

Sigler, Adrian E.

Sims, Larry P.

Skinner, Kenneth W.

Sklodoski, Lawrence

Smith, Bernard E.

Smith, James H.

Smith, Paul L.

Smith, William R.

Soper, Richard O.

Spear, Howard J.

Spitzer, Howard R.

Stephens, Arthur A.

Stevenson, Lawrence

Strauss, Klaus J.

Stroisch, Lord E.

Stutts, Thomas R.

Sutton, Lowhman S.

Swiggum, Larry W.

Tafoya, Joseph E.

Tank, Philip L.

Taylor, William D.

Terry, Philip A.

Thomas, Terence P.

Thompson, Charles C.

Thompson, Onnie Jr.

Torres, Anthony W.

Tracy, Gerald F.

Trier, Kenneth R.

Trusty, William R.

Uecker, David A.

Underwood, Robert S.

Van Horn, Barry W.

Venable, Joseph A.

Virgona, John A.

Vogel, Donald F.

Vossen, Stanley J.

Slifka, John J.

Smith, David W.

Smith, Larry F.

Smith, Robert J.

Soloman, James V.

Sorick, Steven P.

Speer, Louis L.

St. Amand, Richard C.

Stephens, Donald H.

Stiles, Donald L.

Stringfellow, John

Strong, Richard W. J.

Sutton, George S.

Swain, Lee W., Jr.

Szahlender, Julius

Taggart, Larry J.

Taylor, Tommy L.

Tellis, Andrew J.

Thiem, William R.

Thompson, Charlie V.

Thompson, John B.

Thompson, Russell L.

Torres, Lopez Rigob

Treas, Richard L.

Truett, William R.

Turnbull, Robert C.

Umstot, Samuel G., Jr.

Urban, Paul, Jr.

Veihl, John

Ver Pault, Kevin E.

Vitale, William M.

Vonderchek, Walter

Walden, Marion F., Jr.

Ward, Ernest S.

Warthan, Albert W.

Watson, Ronald R.

Wearmouth, Ronald V.

Weeks, Walter D.

Welch, Richard D.

Wescott, Frederick

Whaley, Loy N.

Whitaker, Freddie

White, Whitney L.

Whittington, Russel

Wildman, Melvin A.

Wilkinson, Billie W.

Willey, Donald M., Sr.

Williams, Gerald D.

Williams, John R.

Williams, Lester, Jr.

Williams, Raymond C.

Willison, Loyd M.

Witko, Daniel A.

Wolfe, Richard E.

Wood, Lester L.

Workman, Larry E.

Wright, Booker T.

Wright, Robert J.

Young James M.

Zboyvski, James R.

Ware, Keith L.

Washington, Anthony

Weaks, Timothy H.

Webber, Frederick C.

Weitz, Donald E.

Wentz, Donald R.

West, Robert W.

Whipple, Gary N.

White, Michael D.

Whitehead, Alfred E.

Wieskus, William C.

Wildman, Miles G.

Willard, Kenneth E.

Williams, Alfonzia

Williams, Howard C.

Williams, J. C., Jr.

Williams, Robert F.

Williams, Rossevelt

Wilson, William E.

Wittman, William

Wood, Arthur W.

Woods, Robert W.

Worthington, Edward

Wright, Chester A.

Wright, Robert R., Jr.

Zawisza, Theodore L.

1ST INFANTRY DIVISION
CASUALTIES KILLED IN ACTION

January – December 1969

Acevedo-Millian, Angel. L.

Adams, Leon H.

Adams, Richard L.

Alimo, John C.

Almieda, Joe, Jr.

Ameigh, James K.

Anderson, Buel E.

Anderson, Julian R.

Anderson, Robert L.

Asher, James L.

Atkinson, Francklin G., Jr.

Atwell, Donald W.

Austin, Scotty G.

Baker, George A.

Ballinger, Timothy J.

Barbee, Larry H.

Barnett, Donald E.

Barnett, Steven P.

Barnes, Merrill

Barr, Terry L.

Bartz, Roger C.

Beasley, Edward R.

Benoit, Robert C., Jr.

Bergfeldt, David C.

Beske, William H., Jr.

Bingham, Chester E.

Bird, Dannie L.

Biackburn, William A.

Blakely, Melford K.

Blavat, James N.

Blumer, Kris

Bortle, Jonathan R.

Bowman, Robert E.

Boyd, Charles

Bradbury, Steven W.

Braid, John E.

Breland, Leo M.

Bresnahan, Alan R.

Brewer, Grady L.

Bristol, Clarence F.

Brothen, Robert A.

Brown, Lonnie, Jr.

Brown, Raymond

Brown, William J.

Browne, Walter D.

Buckles, Richard L.

Bullwinkel, Alden J.

Burns, James P.

Burrage, Wayne R.

Buzzard, Lloyd L.

Byers, Easley P., Jr.

Byrd, Reginald T.

Cahagan, James M.

Calandrino, Michael T.

Caldwell, Allen H.

Cama, Dennis R.

Cano, Jose R.

Caraway, Johnnie L.

Carrasco, Aturo

Carroll, Larry D.

Cerrato, Nicolas F.

Chavis, Alphonzo L.

Cheshire, Allen D.

Chevalier, Henry A.

Chiacchio, Joseph S., Jr.

Churchill, Thomas H.

Clark, Bobby D.

Clark, Howe K., Jr.

Clark, James W.

Clarke, Kenneth G., Jr.

Cochrane, Gregg L.

Collins, Thomas R., Jr.

Cook, Charles F.

Cooper, Robert W.

Corrie, Gary A.

Cortez, Juan E.

Cox, Leon D.

Coyle, Gary J.

Craig, Odell

Creason, W. K.

Crist, Stephen E.

Crosby, James E.

Crowlwy, Leland S.

Crum, Steven V.

Crump, Jack V.

Cruz, Enrique S.

Cruz, Luis P.

Cummins, Steven T.

Curran, Daniel J.

Curtis, Roger D.

Cushman, Harold D.

Dabney, Harold T.

Dankowsky, James H.

Darden, William H.

Dasen, Gerald R., III

Davenport, Albert A.

Davison, Jackie L.

Defer, William C.

Deitrick, George D.

Deitz, Thomas M.

Demarcus, Jerry D.

Demings, David E.

Derubeis, Fernando

Diaz, Benito, Jr.

Doebert, Phillip R.

Dominguez, Robert

Downing, James L.

Driggers, Jerry T.

Dukes, Thomas L.

Duffy, James P.

Dugan, Patrick J.

Duggan, Gary L.

Dumont, Roger J.

Dupre, Charles V.

Eder, Robert O.

Edmond, Paul R.

Elam, Walter A.

Elliott, Tommy G.

Enfinger, Kenneth E.

England, Richard A.

Faber, Thomas W.

Farchild, Dennis

Fazzah, George R.

Fernandez, James T.

Fickling, Roy E.

Fields, William M.

Finley, William E.

Firak, Anthony M.

Fitzgerald, Manfred W.

Flaherty, Paul James

Fletcher, Thomas T.

Fralicks, Larry D.

Fleck, Wilbert C.

Fleitman, Glenn R.

Forester, Richard T.

Foster, Dwight D.

Francis, Terrance D.J.

Francisco, Darryl G.

Frankowiak, Robert J.

Farzier, Willie J.

Freeman, Earnest T.

Freeman, Furnace, Jr.

Freestone, David E.

Freepon, John D.

Frericks, Louis W.

Fry, Richard L.

Fulkerson, Robert A.

Gaarder, David E.

Gabbin, Fred L.

Gahagan, James M.

Gaines, James, Jr.

Gant, Herman E.

Garcia, Edward L.

Garcia-Diaz, Juan E.

Garcia, Richard C.

Garrett, Donald W.

Garrick, Jerry A.

Garst, Wallis W.

Garza, David

Gay, James N.

Geiger, Charles R.

Gest, Dennis E.

Geurin, Stephen B.

Gibson, Bruce S.

Gilpin, Jam B.

Giunta, Michael A.

Golden, George K.

Graff, Allen M.

Graham, Johnie L., Jr.

Gray, Ronald L.

Gray, Thomas E.

Green, Dennis J.

Green, Richard H.

Green, Richard L.

Greenwell, Joseph

Greer, Ralph J.

Gregory, William R.

Grissom, Johnny P.

Groom, Alan D.

Grow, Gary W.

Gunter, Alvin F.

Gustafson, Bruce C.

Guthrie, Charles L.

Hall, Clarence J.

Hall, Gary V.

Hamilton, August F.

Hampton, Orville

Harkey, Ronald L.

Harper, Larry N.

Harrell, Stephen C.

Harris, Calvin

Harris, Curtis R.

Harrison, Buffard C.

Harshberger, Eric T.

Harvey, Darnell

Harvey, Lawrence D.

Hausman, Henry R., Jr.

Johnson, Gerald D.

Johnson, Kenneth L.

Johnson, Lorenzo R.

Johnson, Martin R.

Johnson, Russell L.

Jones, Albert J.

Jones, Waymon L., Jr.

Jordan, Orval C.

Kangro, Lauri

Keahey, Carl J.

Kelly, Harvey P.

Kelley, Eddie K.

Kiesler, Raymond J.

Kimbal, Cleatus P.

Kimmell, George S.

King, Donald G.

King, Johnny L.

King, Robert L.

King, Verlon D., Jr.

Kieinau, Carl E.

Klapak, John R., Jr.

Klingensmith, Theodore R.

Kneeland, Paul J.

Knight, Orville L.

Knox, James R.

Kobor, Frank L.

Kolenc, William J.

Korel, Emery L.

Kutschback, Stephen

Labanish, George M.

Landis, Claude B. II

Lawhon, Michael H.

Lehman, Peter A.

Levato, Frank

Laan, Jacob C.

Law, Robert D.

Leake, Ronald J., Jr,

Leap, Thomas E., Jr.

Leming, Charles R.

Lenio, Dale J.

Lennon, Mark S.

Levin, Robert P.

Lewis, Robert B.

Lickey, Michael L.

Leibnitz, James T.

Long, Charles E.

Long, James S.

Long, Ray F.

Longley, Washington M.

Looney, Milford, Jr.

Lopez, Peter

Lopez, Victor

Lucia, Stephen W.

Lyles, Oscar B., Jr.

Lyons, William

Madonna, Dominick J.

Maguire, Calvin G.

Malone, Willie E., Jr.

Manning, John W.

Marconi, Frank J.

Markevitch, Anthony G., Jr.

Marlin, Ellis S.

Marrington, Craig T.

Maske, William J.

Masiak, John J.

Matthews, Bernard J.

McCarty, Brian F.

McCormick, Richard

McDonough, George

McNew, Brian R.

McClung, Wayne D.

McGovern, Michael J.

Meeks, Dustan W.

Melton, Ronald D.

Melvin, James E., Jr.

Mensing, Stanley A.

Mendias, Mario J.

Mercant, Lonnie V.

Milbradt, Dale L.

Miller, Allen R.

Miller, Gary L.

Mitchell, Robert E., Jr.

Mlodzinski, Brumo J.

Mongelli, Alexander A.

Monish, Ronald A.

Moon, Theodore

Moore, Conald E.

Moore, JamesW., Jr.

Moore, Lee E., Jr.

Morgan, Arthur E.

Morrison, James J.

Morrow, James R.

Mosher, Alex R.

Moss, Wiley B.

Mueller, Don R.

Mullins, Stephen R.

Murphy, Dennis J.

Murphy, Joseph T.

Myers, Gene A.

Nakashima, Michael S.

Niederhause, Stephen S.

Nixon, Donald L.

Nohe, Joseph E., Jr.

Nolley, Lee R.

Norvell, Raymond F.

O'Bannion, James R.

Ollikainen, Robert J.

Owen, William L

Parham, John W.

Parker, Danny L.

Parker, Roy E.

Parra, Manuel F.

Parrott, Brian G.

Patrick, Reese M.

Pattison, John Jr.

Pellew, David S.

Pelton, Len E.

Persicke, Allan W.

Peterson, David M.

Peterson, Walter A.

Pettigrew, John F.

Pettigrew, Kenneth D.

Philis, K., Jr.

Pitts, Robert A.

Platt, John H.

Plumlee, James L., Jr.

Poff, Jerry W.

Pollock, Gary J.

Potter, James R.

Pratt, Guy L.,Jr.

Price, Derrill L., Jr.

Proctor, Rickey A.

Propson, Bernard A.

Proudfoot, Timothy C.

Puentes, Miguel A.

Queen, Cecil W.

Quenner, Ulyseses G., Jr.

Quintana, Juan C.

Rapp, Billy W.

Rasmussen, Robert M.

Reel, J. C.

Regan, Philip T., Jr.

Reinel, Russell E.

Renfro, Billy J.

Revis, Hugh E.

Reynolds, William

Rhodes, Donald

Reiderer, Carl J.

Robinson, James M.

Robinson, Joequin

Rodgers, James H.

Rodriguez, Angel L.

Romesser, Richard J.

Roossien, Robert A.

Rosemond, John L.

Rountree, Harvey F., Jr.

Rowe, William E.

Rowles, Steven R.

Rucks, Otis J.

Rush, James T.

Sauers, Gerald

Saunders, John W., Jr.

Sawyer, Bradford

Schimanski, Kenneth A.

Schmitt, Frederick

Schnake, Richard M.

Schultz, Jack E.

Scott, Vernon E.

Sexton, Andrew B.

Sherlock, David H.

Shianna, Louie J.

Shipley, Ronald E.

Siegel, Theodore F.

Siegler, Willie

Sikes, Charles M.

Simpson, Larry D.

Sires, Robert J.

Sizemore, Thomas J.

Slater, James A.

Smith, Aaron C.

Smith, Ariel J.

Smith, Charles E., Jr.

Smith, Donald R.

Smith, Gerral A.

Smith, James W.

Smith, Kenneth W.

Smith, Larry W.

Smith, L. C., Jr.

Smith, Melton E.

Snethen, Robert C.

Spearman, William

Speight, William R.

Spires, Frank

Spilker, James D.

Spurlock, Lon A., II

Stanfield, Gary K.

Steed, William D.

Stevens, Rodney F.

Strouse, Larry D.

Stigen, Wayne D.

Strahan, Walter S.

Strickland, Thomas N.

Stringer, William F.

Stultz, Charles C.

Sullivan, James M.

Sullivan, Thomas H.

Summerlin, John W.

Sweeten, R. C. Earl
Swoner, Ernest W.
Taylor, Clifford M
Taylor, James E.
Taylor, Rudy R.
Taylor, Vincent A.
Tessaro, Michael J.
Thomas, Clyde E.
Thompson, Barry N.
Tidwell, Robert P.
Todtenbier, James L.
Tonan, James R.
Torres, Gilbert G.
Trisdale, Robert L.
Truelove, James M.
Tuck, James W., Jr.
Turner, Rodney C.
Vice, Farrell J.
Virro, Vito
Vad, Henry J.
Vanderbrook, Gary L.
Wagenaar, Daniel
Walker, Leslie E.
Wall, James H.
Wall, James N.
Yewell, Bobby J.
Young, Jerry O.
Youngkrans, Allan T., Jr.
Zapolski, Larry E.

Wallace, Gary A.
Wallace, John E.
Walls, Albert C., Jr.
Walls, John T.
Walters, Richard E.
Walters, William W.
Warfield, Dennis G.
Watson, Kenneth L.
Watson, Richard C.
Webb, Alfred, Jr.
Weiher, Robert L.
Weitzel, Billy D.
West, Paul B.
White, Lenwood, Jr.
Wickward, William K.
Williams, Edgar W., Jr.
Williams, Daniel E.
Williams, Phillip W.
Wilson, Ray G.
Wittman, Robert K.
Wojahn, Arthur E.
Wood, Donald F.
Woods, James R.
Worrell, Robert E.
Yelley, Danny K.

"Thunder

Chief"

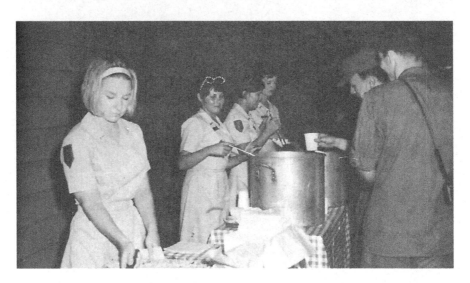

AUTHOR AWARDED

2ND BRONZE STAR

PART TWO

THIS OLD HAT

INTRODUCTION

"This Old Hat" is the narrative experience of the Vietnam veteran as told through the eyes of a ubiquitous veteran's hat.

CHAPTER ONE

I'm just an old hat, but boy do I have some tales to tell! You've probably seen me around town somewhere, proudly sitting atop the head of one of my boys. They'll always be "my boys" to me since I've been with them for more than half a century now. We've been through good times and bad. I know their innermost secrets, the ones that make them scream and wake up in the middle of the night in a cold sweat as the video tape of Vietnam plays over and over in their minds and they clearly see the faces again of friends and comrades who did not survive. I promised I would never reveal what they hide from you, because you might think less of them if you knew. Most of them are pretty good at pushing the monsters back down into the deep recesses of their mind, but eventually it all comes back to the surface. They probably look old, white haired, maybe shuffling along with a cane or riding in a wheelchair, but make no mistake, these men were once strong and mighty warriors, feared by their enemies, loved and respected by their friends. They don't have much to say anymore, but they are always thrilled when you take the time out of your busy day to stop, give them a smile, a handshake or a hug and thank them for their service. Occasionally they see one of their old comrades and are instantly drawn to each other as they warmly shake hands and ask the usual questions. "What year were you there and what outfit were you with?" They share an unbreakable bond only brothers of combat are ever privileged to know. The old memories and emotions of long ago begin to bubble to the surface as their eyes begin to mist over and they exchange goodbyes, moving on quickly with their day, knowing if they linger together too long, the memories will become unbearable. As they move along, often with heads down and backs bent, they instantly snap to attention whenever they hear the sound of the national anthem or the sight of the red, white, and blue flying proudly in the land of freedom. If they hear a jet flying low or the "thump, thump, thump" of a helicopter in the distance, you'll notice their eyes searching the sky as if they were still halfway around the globe, fifty years ago.

A lot of my boys spend their day down at the VA office for medical appointments to get treatment for physical or emotional injuries sustained during their service. Many seek help for emotional issues as they struggle to deal with the memories they have lived with for so long. When they went to the jungles of Vietnam, they were promised by our government their medical needs would be fully met when they returned since they were putting their very lives at risk for America, giving up the very prime of their life. After trudging through the jungles and coming into contact with a "miraculous" new herbicide, agent orange. They were told not to worry, experts had declared it was perfectly safe and it would clear huge blocks of dense jungle, denying the enemy vast sanctuaries. Decades later, after continuing to deny Agent Orange was a deadly chemical, thousands of my boys die each year from horrible cancers, nerve damage and other conditions that have since been proven to have originated from agent orange exposure. Fifty years later now, my boys are still required to file endless paperwork with a mindless bureaucracy, staffed by people who were not yet born when the exposure took place. It often takes years or even decades, undergoing test after test and filing a mountain of paperwork for them to be compensated even a modest amount for their suffering. Many have died waiting for an answer. Even today, they do not make close friends easily, some get angry over seemingly unimportant things, other times they have little patience. They try to cope in different ways, some with alcohol or drugs.

I watched every planeload of vets returning to America from Vietnam. They looked nothing like the smiling, fresh faced boys I saw leaving a year earlier. They looked tired, dirty and depressed with expressionless stares. Their shoulders were slumped over from the burdens they carried in their minds. The Army cleaned them up with a hot shower, a shave, haircut, new uniforms and an all you can eat steak dinner with all the trimmings. Once they were finished processing, they were paid their last, meager pay that included a cheap air fare back home. Then my heart would break each time I witnessed what happened to them at the airport for what should have been a triumphant "Welcome Home". Instead crowds greeted them with disgust, insults, and even spat on them as if they were the lowest of the low. Some of my boys made it to the restroom and changed into civilian clothes, hiding their medals and military uniforms in their bags in an attempt to blend back into a society they could not understand. They were made to feel ashamed to admit they had served so courageously and honorably for America. This period of disrespect for our military will forever be a dark stain in our history, hopefully never to happen again.

CHAPTER TWO

I first met my boys in the 1960's as they entered military service. They came from New York, San Diego, Hawaii, from the Aleutian Islands, Miami and all parts in between. I met them as they entered basic training. It was really something to see how different they were after that first day. Some had long hair, some wore nice clothes and some looked ragged. I heard accents from all over the United States. It didn't take long after getting a GI haircut, a set of fatigues, GI green down to the boxer shorts they wore, and everybody started looking the same. Starting the second day of boot camp, all that individuality was gone and the process of molding these raw recruits into a homogenous fighting team that would respond to orders without question began. They were just kids really. Not long out of grade school, full of life with worlds of vim and vigor. Most were eighteen or nineteen years old but a few were seventeen and needed their parents permission to join. A few lied about their age and were only sixteen. It was fun and exciting to see these kids laughing and joking, innocently thinking they had their whole lives in front of them and were about to embark on a grand adventure. Little did they know their lives would change forever as more than fifty-eight thousand would never make it home again alive. They would soon become battle hardened veterans with their boyish innocence gone forever. Today, I watch the old survivors return for a visit to the long, black granite wall in Washington, D.C with the names of all their fallen buddies etched forever in stone. I see them as their eyes tear over and they wonder why their own names are not on that wall. All my boys suffered from something as a result of their service in a war far from home. Many were forever maimed with missing arms or legs, and most would carry the mental scars to their grave. Untold tens of thousands would die later from exposure to agent orange or other complications of service or from suicide, not able to cope with the memories. I can imagine the VC, (Charlie), saying," Yes, when you were in our country, you killed us with your guns, your bombs and your napalm, but that is not the end of the story. Your own government exposed you to the "orange rain" that has caused you more pain, suffering and death than we ever could have. Even your children and grandchildren will pay a price for what your own country did to you."

My boys were not perfect, but they were the best America had, equal to any fighting force America has ever sent into combat. Many of their school mates fled to Canada, some hid in graduate school, joined the National Guard or used political influence to avoid service. They disgraced themselves and their country and don't deserve to walk the streets with my boys. When America called, my boys stood up proudly and said, "send me". They were the epitome of the motto, "Duty, Honor, Courage."

Looking back, historians debate whether this war was a monumental mistake of judgment or the result of some evil conspiracy by arms manufacturers to make a fortune selling the weapons and ammunition of war. I don't believe there is a clear answer. Politicians always claim credit for success while failures are always laid at the feet of someone else. America's leaders were convinced the free world had to stop the spread of communism and they feared, as outlined in the "Domino Theory", that if communism was allowed to control Vietnam, all of Southeast Asia would soon fall next. However, as in all our wars of the past, America fought for freedom, not for conquest.

My boys served proudly in every military branch. Army, Navy, Air Force, Marines and Coast Guard performed with pride and honor. I was with the naval aviators as they launched from the decks of aircraft carriers such as the USS Oriskany, USS Enterprise, USS Midway and others. They attacked the North Vietnamese factories, roads, bridges and mined the Haiphong harbor to cut off as much support as possible for the North Vietnamese and Viet Cong forces operating in the South. I watched as many of our planes were shot down by the North with the aid of Russian and Chinese supplied anti-aircraft missile systems. The pilots who were able to eject were soon captured and forced to endure years of horrible torture and abuse as they rotted in jail. At the same time, Jane Fonda visited nearby to deliver aid and support to the enemy. Some were captured in Laos or Cambodia and were held in small bamboo cages as if they were animals. Many were never heard from again.

My Marines in the I Corps area around the strategic cities of Hue and Danang fought a North Vietnamese enemy that was determined, well-trained, well-armed and relentless in their attacks. The valor of those young men was equal to any ever displayed by an American fighting force.

In the Mekong Delta of South Vietnam, my boys patrolled the rivers and waterways of the rice belt in their sleek attack boats that were heavily armed, trying to deny the enemy their food staple, rice. They would patrol for days with no enemy contact, then when they least expected it, a fierce battle would occur as they sailed into an ambush. Later, the enemy would vanish into the thick jungle as if they were never there.

Further North, elements of the 101st Infantry Division made contact with the enemy on May 10th, 1969 at hill 937 while conducting a sweep of the A Shau Valley. The size and strength of the enemy force was at first unknown. The battle that ensued was known as the "Battle at Hamburger Hill." My boys were ordered to attack from the bottom of the hill and drive the enemy off. Their first attack was met with overwhelming resistance and they were driven back down the hill. Reinforcements were called in and the battle raged for more than 10 days as they attempted one attack after another, only to be repelled time after time, taking more casualties on each attempt. Some days they fought in relentless monsoon rains that were followed by intense heat and humidity. Boys with only minor wounds were ordered to continue attacking while their buddies fell around them, dead or dying from the constant machine gun and small arms fire from above. Air Force Phantom jets roared overhead, dropping their bomb loads and napalm cannisters. The concussions often caused eardrums to rupture and blood drained down their necks while the searing heat from the napalm seemed to destroy everything in its path, literally sucking the air from their lungs. Dozens of my boys died there and hundreds more suffered arms or legs being torn from their body as they screamed for help. They cried out to their buddies, to God and begged for their mothers and the mercy of morphine to help ease the almost unbearable pain. Eventually, the hill was captured by the 101st at the price of several hundred dead or wounded. After occupying the position for a few days and destroying their food, weapons or ammunition, the 101st was ordered to abandon the hill and proceed on to a new mission. Shortly after the 101ˢᵗ departed, the hill was again occupied by North Vietnamese troops.

Men of the 1ˢᵗ Infantry Division in central Vietnam patrolled the jungles day after day, crossing streams and waterways in pursuit of the enemy, often having to stop and remove leeches they picked up in the polluted water. Many days were uneventful, then suddenly they were attacked in a fierce ambush attack. They had to constantly be searching the path ahead for booby traps or stepping into a punji stick trap where the tips were smeared with water buffalo dung to infect the wounds. The enemy would attack, then vanish into the jungle or an underground tunnel system where they could hide and pop up in another area. Weary from the physical and emotional exertion along with a lack of sleep or decent food, they somehow continued to put one foot in front of the other.

I saw the bravery of the helicopter crews as they set down time after time into a hot landing zone to take wounded GIs on board for emergency aid until they reached the hospital. After landing and unloading their cargo, they would often have to spray the inside of the chopper with water to wash the blood from inside that was streaming out the doors onto the tarmac below. Inside the hospital, doctors and nurses worked tirelessly to save as many as possible. Young nurses tried to comfort them with assurances they would not die, then go outside and weep because they knew many would never survive. I saw the young USO and red cross girls give them a gentle female touch and listen patiently as they tried to give comfort to my boys.

CHAPTER THREE

F ast forward to the present day. My boys are not whiners or mired in self-pity. They are however, proud of their service, when they were willing to lay down their lives for their comrades and their country. Many did just that even when it was popular to oppose the war. I overheard one of my boys recently telling his friend about his experience with the 1st Infantry Division in Vietnam. He was only eighteen years old at the time. He jumped out of a Huey helicopter into what seemed like a quiet landing zone. His platoon moved out toward a tree line about three hundred yards away and proceeded cautiously into the jungle. A short time later, he was hit in the head and immediately fell to the ground, seemingly dead. He said he could not move or speak, but he was aware of what was happening around him and could hear his buddies talking with each other. His buddies thought he was dead, but they refused to leave him there in the jungle. Instead, they carried his seemingly dead body to a dust-off chopper for extraction. The medics thought he was dead so they focused their attention on other wounded GIs. When they arrived at the aid station, medical personnel thought he was dead also, but one young nurse recognized a sign of life in him. Because of that, he survived his wounds. Today, he wears a black patch over his eye, the right side of his head is mangled and he has suffered through constant pain as a result. I was struck with amazement and admiration as he said, "If I were put in the same circumstances again, I would make the same decision to serve my country, even knowing what the outcome would be."

Time has healed many of the wounds suffered fifty years ago and America has indeed come to recognize the bravery, suffering and patriotism of these young men as they shared their life changing experience. They ate together, slept together, laughed and cried together, fought together and sometimes died together. I wish they all could have received the honor and respect they should have received when they came home, but for those still living, it is truly sometimes overwhelming. My brave boys have finally been given the honor and respect they deserve.

I often wonder if America learned any lessons from this tragedy. I know many young men came to know Jesus during those days in the midst of terrible evil around them, and for that I am grateful.

Now as I look around America, I see hats of a new generation of warrior. They represent different wars and battlegrounds, Iraq and Afghanistan, but the young men have not changed. They are all young, strong and include the finest men America can produce. America has been blessed by God in order to represent Him in the world by being a force for good and freedom. There will always be another foe to face, another battle to fight, and thank God, there will be another American soldier to fight it.

Yes, I'm just an old hat, but I will never forget my boys. Whenever you hear someone complain about America, or disrespect the flag or our national anthem, remind them of my boys and what they did to give another generation of Americans the freedom we often just take for granted.

See you around town!

CHAPTER FOUR

Most of my boys have made it back home now, many in caskets with their names etched on the black granite walls of the Vietnam Memorial in Washington, D.C. They will be forever remembered as young and full of life, with no more pain and suffering to endure. They never witnessed the disrespect and shame their comrades experienced returning home to an ungrateful country. Many however, have never made it back home and their fates are unknown.

Fifty years later, things have made a complete turnaround. Two new generations of Americans have come to realize the courage, patriotism and sacrifice my boys demonstrated so long ago. My boys have finally received the long overdue respect and appreciation they deserve. Millions of Americans have come together to honor them through charitable and patriotic organizations like The Wounded Warrior Project, Quilts of Honor, and the Honor Flight program.

The Honor Flights chapters are one hundred percent staffed by volunteers and are funded with private donations. Once a year each local chapter leads a group of about one hundred fifty veterans of World War II, The Korean War and the Vietnam War on an exciting, emotionally charged visit to Washington, D.C.

The local chapter in Brunswick, Georgia led their group in May 2018. The vets gathered at the Brunswick, Georgia airport at 5:00 AM full of excitement, wearing the uniform of the day, a blue tee shirt and me, This Old Hat. The feeling of comradeship they shared as survivors of combat so long ago, came rushing back. Each one had an escort accompany them since so many were in wheelchairs or needed other assistance traveling. Hundreds of people gathered to greet my boys with cheering and clapping for them as they filed through the airport and boarded their plane for the flight to Baltimore, Maryland and a bus ride into Washington, D.C. The Brunswick airport fire department honored them with a water cannon salute as the plane rolled down the runway.

The flight to Baltimore was filled with laughter and reminded me of the flight home from Vietnam. It was good to see my boys finally receiving the honor and respect they earned and to see them filled with pride and joy.

Arriving in Baltimore, my boys were greeted with a military honor guard at the airport gate and loud cheers and applause as they proudly made their way through the building to the buses awaiting them. They all seemed to try and stand straight and tall, even though the years have left most a little slumped over. After boarding the buses for the ride into Washington, they were led by a National Park Service escort complete with flashing lights and sirens screaming, parting the heavy early morning traffic headed into the nation's capitol, stopping for nothing, not even traffic lights. A hero's welcome greeted them all the way.

The first stop of the day was at the World War II memorial where they were met by pretty young girls dressed in costumes of the 1940s, planting big, red lipstick kisses on each one. One old vet in a wheelchair stated he would not wash the lipstick off his face for a week! Next, they were off to the Vietnam Memorial Wall, probably the most emotional stop of the day. Standing in front of that wall brought back a flood of memories of times past and close friends lost in combat long ago. The same unspoken question on everyone's mind was, why did I survive and my buddies did not? Why is his name up there and mine is not?

Other stops included the Korean Memorial, the Navy Memorial and the Marines of Iwo Jima Memorial. Another memorable stop was a visit to Arlington National Cemetery as they gathered to watch the changing of the guard at the tomb of the unknown soldier, guarded twenty-four hours each day, during good weather and bad by the elite Tomb Sentinels of the "Old Guard". The row after row of white marble headstones marking the final resting place of thousands of heroes of all American wars reminded us of the unbreakable bond shared by all American soldiers.

After a very long, but exciting day, my boys boarded their chartered plane for the ride back to Brunswick when they were surprised with a "mail call". Each vet's name was called and he received a large envelope, filled with letters from friends and family expressing appreciation and gratitude for his service.

Landing at Brunswick around 9:00 PM, they were greeted again with a military honor guard, a band played patriotic music as thousands of well-wishers cheered, waving American flags and hand-made placards expressing appreciation for their service. Wives greeted husbands with hugs and kisses and strangers from all walks of life shook hands and patted them on the back. Young school children, who were well past their bed times, came with their families to greet the old soldiers and give them thanks and notes of appreciation.

This special day was finally over, but it was the day my boys deserved so long ago and every American hero deserves today. I did not see a single one who was not overcome with emotion and gratitude at some point in the day, trying to hold back the tears.

That's it for now, but I'll see you around!!

This Old Hat.

Made in the USA
Las Vegas, NV
24 November 2020